Tu

Thrace, Black Sea Coast, West, South and Central Anatolia

CONTENTS

Part 1

This is Turkey 3
Holidays in Turkey 4
Essential details in brief 6
The Turkish way of life 7
Turkey and Islam 8
Agriculture and Industry 9
Signposts of History 11
Phases of History 12
For the Art lover 15
Food and drink 17

Part 2

Hints for your holiday 18

Where to go and what to see 19
Thrace and Istanbul 19
Bosporus, Sea of Marmara and the Dardanelles 31
Black Sea Coast 40
Aegean Coast and Hinterland 42
South Anatolian Coast 61
Central Anatolia 74

Part 3

Useful things to know 90
Before you go 90
Getting to Turkey 90
During your stay 91

Making yourself understood 95

Index 96

Maps and Plans
Town plan of Istanbul 22
Dardanelles 32
Town plan of Bursa 35
Pergamon 43
Aegean Coast 45
Town plan of Izmir 46
Ephesus and Selçuk 51
South-west Turkey 55

South Anatolian Coast 62
Town plan of Antalya 65
Central Anatolia 75
Capadocia 79
Tuff region 82
Town plan of Ankara 85
General map of Turkey back cover

Antalya

This is Turkey

'Come to the land of magnificent mosques with slender minarets reaching high into the Anatolian sky, to the colourful, aromatic, alluring, magical world of the bazaars, to sultans' palaces, treasure houses filled with a dazzling wealth of gold and precious stones, to mighty Seljuk, Crusader and Byzantine fortresses, to ruined temples, theatres and baths recalling a brilliant Greek and Roman past, to the remains of an ancient Hittite culture, and — by Allah — to the very oldest city in the world. Enjoy the hospitality of a people to whom the British are friends, savour Arab specialities with quaint names such as *To His Majesty's taste* or *The Iman fainted,* treat yourself to delicious Turkish pastries. Gaze in wonder at the petrified cascades of Pamukkale, at the thundering waterfalls, the grottos, ravines and mountains, and at the strange tuff landscape of Cappadocia with its hidden rock churches and rock dwellings. Breathe woodland fragrances and delight in a profusion of cherry and apricot blossom, mimosa, crocuses and wild azaleas. Swim in the crystal clear waters of the Aegean, find yourself again in the solitude of the woods and coves, and walk on the expanse of soft, white sand once trodden by Cleopatra.'

This is how an invitation to visit Turkey might sound in the wonderfully expressive language of the Near East.

Visitors who accept the invitation should not however expect the kind of organised tourism found in the holiday areas of Spain, Italy and France. Don't be surprised if cleanliness and service are not up to British standards — the toilets in some restaurants are incredibly primitive; buses and flights tend to run late, often the air-conditioning doesn't work, and goats, donkeys and sheep hold up the traffic. Nor can you count on English being spoken everywhere.

Turkey has done a lot to promote tourism in recent years. Modern hotels and holiday villages have sprung up, there are now good roads linking nearly all the important towns, and there is also good road access to most of the tourist attractions, to which, as a rule, excursions can be made by bus.

Nevertheless Turkey remains an exotic country, whose people have different cultural and religious values, and for whom the modern period began only 60 years ago with Atatürk. Before this the Turks still used the Arabic script, wore veils and turbans and later the fez, and sold their daughters into marriage. They had no family names, only first names such as Ali or Mustafa, or a nickname like 'Hare with the skinny legs'. The men, or 'masters', rode on donkeys while the women walked submissively behind carrying the loads, as in rural areas they still do.

Yet the charm of Turkey lies precisely in this otherness, in its mixture of tradition and faltering progress, in its natural contrasts and wonderfully unspoiled scenery, in the extraordinary hospitality of its people which can be so daunting to the guest, and in the sense of adventure which travellers in Turkey can still sometimes experience. If you are happy to marvel at what you see, if you are willing to project yourself into this other world and to view things through the eyes of a people who place their fate in the hands of Allah the Almighty, then you will love Turkey — *Insha'allah,* God willing.

Holidays in Turkey

Turkey today offers the most varied choice of holidays.

Cultural holidays. An almost inexhaustible cultural richness makes Turkey the ideal destination for an educational holiday, whether you travel with an organised tour or on your own.

Centres for study holidays are Troy, Pergamon, Izmir (Smyrna), Ephesus, Priene, Miletus and Didyma on the Aegean coast, Hierapolis and Aphrodisias inland, and Halikarnassos, Xanthos, Termessos, Perge, Aspendos and Side on the 'Turkish Riviera'. Cappadocia is another area of special historical interest, with its numerous rock churches and underground cities which once provided Christian communities with places of refuge from attack. Finally there is Ankara, with its extraordinary archaeological museum and, of course, Istanbul.

Besides these major centres there are many other sites scattered all over the country with archaeological remains dating from various periods. They are well worth visiting, though a little pioneering spirit may be needed to get you there. Such expeditions can give the visitor a sense of genuine exploration and provide experiences which are both novel and unique. They can also make you realise how useful it is to speak some French as well as English!

Beach holidays. A combined beach and cultural holiday is an ideal way of making the most of a visit to Turkey. While it is possible to hire a car in the larger tourist centres, the cultural part of any holiday is already well catered for by the many excursions organised from the main seaside resorts.

In the coastal resorts themselves surf-boarding, water-skiing and sailing are widely available. The best season for sailing is from May to September although in mid-summer a strong north-westerly wind, the *meltemi,* can blow over the Aegean. There are large, well-equipped marinas in Çeşme, Kuşadasi, Bodrum, Kaş, Antalya, Kemer and Alanya, mostly with cafés, restaurants and shops. For more details see the leaflet 'Yachting in Turkey' obtainable from the Turkish Tourist and Information Office (address on page 94).

Sub-aqua diving is only permitted in a few places, partly due to the lack of life-saving services but also in order to stop the sea-bed antiquities being plundered. Since the restrictions in force at any time can change it is advisable to make enquiries from the Turkish Tourist and Information Office before you leave. Spear-fishing and underwater hunting in general is forbidden. Snorkelling on the other hand is freely allowed and is often quite delightful. There are specially designated areas where sea, river and lake fishing is permitted and where fishing for sport requires no special licence. There are however regulations concerning the kind of equipment to be used, the size of fish which may be landed, and size of catch.

Activity holidays. Many resorts have tennis courts and minigolf and in some places riding provides an additional attraction. There are also holiday clubs catering specially for the sports enthusiast. Robinson Club Camyuva near Kemer and Club Pamfiliya near Side, for example, both offer archery in addition to watersports, and Pamfiliya has facilities for weight training.

Turkey offers plenty of scope for mountaineering and hill walking. In the western half of Anatolia, Hasandagi (3250 m), south of Aksaray, and the extinct volcano Erciyes Dagi (3916 m), south of Kayseri, are among the mountains which can be tackled by the less experienced climber.

Although the many mountains ranging from 2000 to 5000m in height provide more than enough winter snow, skiing in Turkey remains relatively undeveloped. Ulu Dag near Bursa and Köroğludaği south of Bolu are among the very few resorts with prepared pistes, ski-lifts, ski-hire and instruction.

Turkey also has a number of spas, some of which (e.g. Bursa, Çeşme, Pamukkale) have thermal springs. While the health resorts provide a variety of therapeutic treatments, facilities generally speaking are not yet fully geared to the requirements of an international clientele.

Essential details in brief

Name: Türkiye Cumhuryeti (Republic of Turkey).

Declared a Republic: October 29th 1923.

Area: 708,580 sq. km (nearly 3 times the size of the United Kingdom); 97% is in Asia Minor or Anatolia (*anadolu* means orient), and 3% in European Turkey (Thrace). 55% of the total area lies above 1000 m (Ararat — Agri Dagi — 5167 m).

Frontiers: Land frontiers with Syria, USSR, Iraq, Iran, Bulgaria and Greece. 7205 km of mainland coastline (excluding islands).

Population: Excluding Turks living abroad, 51.4 million, according to the 1985 census. (United Kingdom 54 million, 1981 census.)

Population groups: About 95% Turkish stock. Minority groups include Kurds, Arabs, Armenians, and Greeks.

Religion: 98% Muslims, of whom 90% are Sunnites.

Official language: Turkish: Latin characters replaced the Arabic alphabet in 1928.

Capital: Ankara: population 2.3 million. (Largest city: Istanbul, population 6 million.)

Constitution: Secular national democratic republic. The President is General Kenan Evren. Executive power is exercised by the President of the Republic and the Council of Ministers. Sovereignty lies in the Grand National Assembly *(Türkiye Büyük Miletus Meclisi)* which has 400 elected delegates.

Administrative divisions: 67 provinces, each with a governor appointed by the executive.

Chief exports: Cotton, wool (also fabrics), tobacco, fruit and chromite.

Chief imports: Machines, chemical products and motor vehicles.

Time: Turkey is in the Eastern European Time Zone, 2 hours ahead of Greenwich Mean Time (London 10 a.m. = Ankara 12 noon).

The Turkish way of life

There is no simple way to characterise a whole nation, and 50 million Turks are no exception. As well as differences in wealth and social status, the great diversity of Turkish life reflects the contrasts between towns and countryside, between east and west, and between the coastal and inland areas of Anatolia.

In a Turkish bath

Nevertheless some generalisations are possible. Private life in Turkey, for example, is marked by a strong sense of commitment to the family — and not merely to the immediate family — guaranteeing aid and protection to its members; even when grown up, children retain very close ties with their parental home. In public men are invariably treated as superiors, but in the home it is mother who holds sway. In lower and middle class families a foreign daughter-in-law, never exactly welcomed with open arms, is liable to be treated as an inferior. Owning a house, or in town a flat, no matter how small, is essential to the Turk's happiness and he is willing to work for years to afford one. Yet even a Turk's best friends seldom enter his private domain. He much prefers to invite people out to a restaurant, especially if his home is too small for festive entertaining. Engagements, weddings, birthdays and circumcisions are celebrated at great expense in restaurants or hotels.

Even today, in small towns and villages the coffee-houses are only patronised by men, while unaccompanied women frequent the western-style *pastahane* (cafés). In the bazaar *(çarşi)* where both men and women engage in selling, customers of both sexes are treated equally. The service sector and catering on the other hand remain predominantly male preserves.

Owing to western influences the role of women in public life has changed considerably during the last 50 years. Women teachers, judges, secretaries, politicians and policewomen are an indispensable part of professional life. In the large cities every fifth lawyer and every sixth doctor is a woman, working self-confidently in a man's world. Yet on the land women are still labouring in the fields supervised by those men who happen not to be in the *cayhane* (tea-house) indulging their passion for board-games. In almost all rural areas women, often carrying heavy loads, walk behind the men riding donkeys. The practice of arranged marriages and the old custom of buying a bride still survive, especially in the east and south-east of the country.

In general the picture is one of striking contrasts: suicidal manoeuvres in traffic combined with extreme courtesy in everyday life; a willingness to help that never ceases to amaze and an almost excessive hospitality, together with suspicion and reserve towards strangers and the unfamiliar; also a stoic calm and composure in

Turkish folk-dancers

the face of danger and catastrophe. In a country afflicted by earthquakes the people just keep rebuilding their homes, knowing only too well that *kismet* (fate) may well bring bad luck yet again.

The Republic of Turkey's programme of secularization has still not reached all corners of the country and most people remain religious, although religious orthodoxy with its associated intolerance has been forced to yield considerable ground. Nowadays even the tourist can enter a mosque during prayers, though care should be taken not to walk between someone praying and the *mihrab* (prayer niche) as this would invalidate the prayer. Appropriate clothing should also, of course, be worn by visitors to a mosque; shorts and mini-skirts are not acceptable and women are required to wear a headscarf and cover their shoulders.

Turkey and Islam

In contrast to many other Islamic countries, religion and state are strictly separated in Turkey. This principle, together with those of religious freedom and freedom of conscience, is firmly enshrined in the 1982 Constitution, although the reintroduction of religion as a compulsory subject in schools is in conflict with it. Since the Second World War Islam has gained ground worldwide, so it is not surprising that Turkey, a strictly Islamic empire until the time of Atatürk, has been carried with the tide.

Like Christianity, Islam, meaning *submission to God,* acknowledges only one God. Its founder Mohammed (A.D. 570-632), Allah's prophet, was born in Mecca, his revelations being written down in the *Koran*, the Holy Book of Islam. A.D. 622, the year of Mohammed's flight to Medina, is year nought in the Islamic calendar. Islam provided the Arab peoples with a unifying bond, and within a few decades of its foundation had spread over large areas, securing for Mohammed an important place in world history.

Like Christianity Islam has been divided by schism into different sects. 90% of Turks are *Sunnites*, as are the majority of Muslims. *Sunna* means tradition and the Sunnites conform strictly to the practices and pronouncements of the prophet. In contrast to the smaller, less tolerant *Shiite* sect (*shia* = sect) the Sunni Muslims recognise caliphs (successors) not directly descended from Mohammed. The Shiites on the other hand, who are now themselves divided into several different groups (Imanites, Ismailites, Zaidites etc.) only recognise as true caliphs the descendants of Mohammed's son-in-law, Ali.

Devout Turks, particularly those living abroad, still observe four of the five duties of Islam: to confess faith through prayer (*salat*) five times a day, to give alms, to fast in the month of Ramadan (Turkish *Ramazan*) and to make a pilgrimage to Mecca, after which the pilgrim may take the title *Hajji*. A fifth duty in former days was to participate in the war against the infidel, or non-believer.

Nowadays the *muezzin* usually issues the call to prayer over a loudspeaker, the faithful gathering in the mosque (*cami*) or outside in the open air. At the entrance to every mosque is a fountain where, before praying, faces, hands, armpits and feet are washed. On Fridays, the Islamic sabbath, large numbers will make their way into the mosque, or congregate in the square in front. The *iman* who is not a professional priest but a pious member of the community, leads the prayers from the pulpit (*mimber*) while the congregation kneels facing in the direction of Mecca, indicated by the position of the prayer niche (*mihrab*). During prayers a variety of different postures have to be assumed. Traditionally a Koranic school (*medrese*) and charity kitchen (*imaret*) would be attached to the mosque, and often a hospital, an old people's home and a library as well. Traditionally also, and still today, people meet at the fountain in the inner courtyard of the mosque to rest and talk before or after prayers.

Despite the widespread allegiance to Islam, constitutionally Turkey is not an Islamic state, as is evident from the beer, wine, raki and pork consumed in the cities, and the role of women in public life. There is however a trend towards stricter adherence to Islamic traditions, with more and more restaurants, for example, no longer serving alcohol.

Agriculture and Industry

During the early years of the Republic Turkey under Atatürk had a planned economy, but following the Second World War greater freedom from controls was introduced in an effort to create a more vigorous, restructured economy and to develop new markets. It is only in recent years however that there has been fundamental progress in modernisation with the lifting of restrictions on imports, the encouragement of foreign investment and the privatisation of state industries. An important factor contributing to economic growth has been the emergence of a more highly trained industrial workforce capable of passing on its skills, mainly the result of workers returning from abroad to work at home.

Even so Turkey remains primarily an agricultural country which could soon find itself facing a shortage of utilisable farmland to feed its growing population. To counter this threat steps are being taken to develop more intensive forms of agriculture by building dams to improve irrigation, increasing the production of fertilisers and farm machinery and the establishment of farming co-operatives. The main crops, all of which are sold on the international market, are cereals, sugar beet, cotton, tobacco, fruit, vegetables, nuts, olives, tea and wine. Livestock farming is also an increasingly important sector in Turkish agriculture.

The population distribution has altered considerably over the last few decades with 50% now living in the towns and cities compared to only 20% in the 1950s. This exodus from the countryside is scarcely beneficial to agriculture and leads to increasing numbers of urban unemployed, which in turn fuels social unrest. At the same time industry has been expanding. Turkey possesses rich mineral deposits including borax, chromium, copper, lignite, oil and iron ore, which are exported as raw materials in addition to being processed at home. Important contributions to the economy are made by textiles, involving the export of half-finished and finished goods, and the construction industry which undertakes design and building work abroad, mostly in the Near East. Tourism is expanding rapidly and the Turkish economy is scarcely able to keep pace with the demand for a stable infrastructure which the growing tourist industry requires. The benefits of growth in tourism however are very visible in related sectors such as the manufacture of carpets, copperware and leather goods, handicrafts and textiles.

With industrialisation the gap between town and country has widened, as has the gulf between the large landowner and the peasant farmer who, with three goats tethered behind a mud hovel and a wooden plough, has no chance of catching up with the modern world. Many villagers find themselves working as labourers for the rich land-owning farmers. Modernisation is proceeding slowly, particularly in the eastern region, due in large measure to people clinging to old customs and traditions but in part also to the influence of Islamic fundamentalism.

National speciality

Shopping for bargains in the market

About 2000–1200 B.C. Hittite Empire (the Hittites were an Indo-European people whose capital was Hattuşa, now Boğazkale).

1200–1000 Greek settlements on the west coast of Asia Minor and later cities also on the Black Sea coast.

9th–7th c. Urartu Kingdom around Lake Van. Phrygian Kingdom in Central Anatolia with its capital at Gordion. From 600 B.C. the Armenians, an Indo-European people, establish themselves in the former Urartu territories.

7th/6th c. Western Asia Minor is dominated by the kingdom of Lydia, except for the Lycians in the far south west.

From the mid-6th c. The Persians conquer Asia Minor. Wars between Greeks and Persians continue intermittently until the 4th c. B.C.

334/333 Alexander the Great conquers most of Asia Minor. His death is followed by the struggle between the 'Diodochoi' (successors).

From 281 The Seleucid Empire extends across most of Asia Minor.

1st c. A.D. The Romans conquer the whole of Asia Minor.

330 Byzantium (Constantinople) becomes the capital of the Roman Empire.

395 Division of the Roman Empire into eastern and western empires.

From 7th c. The Arabs threaten the Byzantine (eastern) Empire.

8th/9th c. The Arabs overrun large parts of Asia Minor. From the mid-9th c. Byzantium regains control of Asia Minor, Syria and Palestine.

1071 Seljuk victory at Manzikert (Malazgirt). Anatolia comes under Seljuk (Turkish) domination. Ikonian (Konya) becomes the capital in 1092.

11th/12th c. During the Crusades power passes back and forth between the two sides.

1258 Mongol invasion. Collapse of the Seljuk Empire.

1281 The Turkish Ottoman ruler Osman I extends his territory in Anatolia and founds the Ottoman Empire.

14th c. The Ottomans conquer Serbia and Greece. Constantinople is besieged by the Turks. The Byzantine capital is transferred to Brussa (Bursa), then to Adrianopel (Edirne).

1453 Constantinople falls to Mehmet II. As Istanbul it becomes the capital of the Ottoman Empire. End of the Byzantine Empire.

16th c. Ottoman conquest of Iraq, Syria, Armenia, Belgrade, Rhodes and Budapest under Selim I and Suleiman I. First siege of Vienna 1529. Under Suleiman the empire reaches the height of its power.

1683 Second unsuccessful attack on Vienna.

1717 Prince Eugene defeats the Turks at Belgrade.

1717–1914 Wars against Austria, France and Russia. Slow demise of the Ottoman (Turkish) Empire: War of Greek Independence; Russian expansionism; Egypt becomes a British protectorate; the other North African possessions are ceded to France and Italy; loss of the Balkans except for Thrace; Cyprus ceded to Britain.

1914–1918 In World War I Turkey fights on the side of Germany as an ally of the Central Powers.

1919 Greek invasion of Turkey. Struggle for national independence under Atatürk. Crushing defeat of the Greek army in 1922.

1923 Turkey is declared a republic with Atatürk as the first president. End of the Ottoman Empire.

1924 Comprehensive reforms on western lines. Abolition of the caliphate.

1939–1945 Turkey remains neutral in World War II (formal declaration of war on Germany in 1945).

1946 Introduction of a multi-party system.

1952 Turkey joins NATO.

1982 A new Turkish constitution is introduced.

Phases of History

Few if any other parts of the world have been the homeland of so many different peoples and the cradle of so many different cultures as Asia Minor, forming as it does the land-bridge between Asia and Europe. Greek, Roman, Mesopotamian, Persian, Indian, Arabic, south Russian and even Chinese remains are found here. The earliest archaeological finds, relics of a still unidentified people, date from the 6th millennium before Christ (see Catal Höyük and Hacilar).

The first people known to us by name are the Hittites who founded the 'Hittite Empire' (capital: Hattuşa) around 2000 B.C. This empire collapsed about 1200 B.C. under the onslaught of various tribes, following which Asia Minor became divided amongst several different peoples including, from Europe, the Phrygians, Lydians, Lycians and Carians, and also the Greeks who came and settled in western and central Anatolia during the 'Dorian Migration'.

The Phrygians and later the Lydians were the founders of great empires (9th—6th c. B.C.), and to this day the wealth of rulers such as King Midas of Phrygia and King Croesus (Kroisos) of Lydia are legendary. The Urartians, an invading tribe from the east, also succeeded in founding an empire around Lake Van. The Greek colonists established city-states which reached their cultural and economic heyday in the 7th and 6th centuries B.C.

During the 8th and 7th centuries B.C. the kingdoms of Phrygia and Urartu collapsed following invasion by the Cimmerians and Scythians from the Indo-European steppes. The Lydian Empire, which included the Greek colonies, survived however until the 6th c. B.C. when the Persians conquered the whole of Asia Minor. Persian sovereignty over the Greek cities in Anatolia was the cause of the intermittent conflict with mainland Greece which was to continue for hundreds of years ('the Persian Wars').

Alexander the Great and the Diadochoi (4th and 3rd c. B.C.)

Persian domination was finally broken when Alexander the Great swept across western Asia. Except for some northern outposts, such as Bithynia in the north-west, Asia Minor became part of a huge empire extending as far as India. Following Alexander's death his generals fought amongst themselves for possession of the territories, and Anatolia became involved in the 'Diadochoi conflicts' (Greek *diadoche* = successor), eventually falling, almost in its entirety, into the hands of the powerful Seleucid dynasty. Only Pergamon emerged as an independent kingdom.

The Romans (2nd c. B.C.–4th c. A.D.)

Rome had meanwhile developed to take its place among the great powers. The Greek territories in Anatolia had already been annexed around 200 B.C. with the help of the king of Pergamon. In 133 B.C. Pergamon itself became a Roman province when the ruler bequeathed his kingdom to Rome, and a little over 200 years later the whole of Asia Minor had been incorporated in the Roman Empire.

The vastness of the empire created problems. In the upheaval caused by the migration of the tribes it became clear that it could no longer be governed centrally. When in A.D. 330 Constantine the Great transferred his seat of government to Byzantium, the 'New Rome', it was only a matter of time before a split occurred. In 395 the Roman Empire was divided into a western and an eastern territory, with the capital of the latter at 'Constantinople' as the 'New Rome' was soon called.

3-figured Hatti god-symbol from the Anatolian Art Museum, Ankara

While the west succumbed a few decades later to invasion by the Germanic tribes, the eastern empire survived for more than a thousand years.

The Byzantine Empire (A.D. 395–1493)

After Imperium Romanum was divided its cultural and political centre shifted to the east, which, with the growth of Greek influence in the 7th c., became known as the 'Byzantine Empire'.

Ever since the foundation of Christianity Asia Minor had found itself destined to play an important role in the development of the religion, and even after the death of Constantine it was there that many major religious issues were decided. The Councils of the Christian Church were held either in Constantinople or in Asia Minor until the 9th c. Of special consequence was the Council of Chalcedon held in 451. Its decision to confer the same authority on the bishop of Constantinople as was wielded by the bishop of Rome resulted in a long drawn-out dispute within the Church.

The Byzantine Empire was increasingly involved in defensive wars — with the Slavs, Langobards, Persians and Bulgarians — sometimes bringing success but frequently defeat. It also proved unable to prevent the invasion of its territory by the Arabs following the death of Mohammed in 632, and Constantinople itself had to be defended against several (unsuccessful) Arab attacks. In the 8th c. large parts of Asia Minor were temporarily under Arab control, though by the 9th and 10th centuries Byzantium had gained new strength and was able to recapture its former territories in Asia Minor, Syria and Palestine. At the start of the new millennium however the Byzantine army and navy were to prove inadequate for the defence of the empire against its next adversaries, the Turks.

The Turks (from the 11th c. A.D.)

'The Turks' were a group of related tribes whose homeland was inland Asia, some living by tilling the soil and some as nomadic herdsmen. The latter were a warlike people, continually engaged in plundering and conquest, and it was they who encountered the world of Islam for the first time in north-eastern Iran. Joining forces initially with the Muslim armies, the Turkomans, as they were called, quickly seized control of large areas of territory.

By the 10th and 11th centuries the Seljuks, a powerful tribe named after one of their leaders Seljuk, had emerged to rule over a Turkoman Empire extending from India to the Caspian Sea. As Muslims they took upon themselves the role of 'guardians' of Sunnite orthodoxy, their policy of conquest over the lands of the Shiite minority leading eventually to an expansion north-westward into Asia Minor. Victory over the Byzantines at Malazgirt in 1071 established a Turkish presence in the region and in the following decades the Seljuk empire of 'Rum' was created in eastern and central Anatolia, with its capital at Ikonion (Konya).

At intervals from 1100 onwards the Christian Crusaders from western Europe arrived in Jerusalem with their armies, and though at first they allied themselves with the Byzantines to fight the Seljuks, conflicts soon broke out between the two Christian forces. The Crusaders established their own enclaves in Asia Minor and in 1204 captured Constantinople itself, following which, for a period of 50 years, the Byzantine Empire became fragmented into numerous small principalities. The Turks in Asia Minor took advantage of Byzantine weakness to bring large areas of the Mediterranean and Black Sea coasts under their control. To the east, where the powerful Seljuk empire had also begun to disintegrate, the boundaries of 'Turchia' were extended as far as Ararat, creating a realm which grew and flourished until the Mongol invasions in the mid-13th c., when Asia Minor once again broke up into a number of small states.

The Ottoman Empire (1281–1923)

Osman (pronounced Othman in Arabic, from which the term Ottoman derives) was ruler of one of the small states which emerged following the Mongol invasions. With military ingenuity and political shrewdness he succeeded in securing control of Asia Minor, founding a dynasty which was to reign until 1923 and an empire which was to cast its threatening shadow over Europe for several centuries.

Osman's successors were able to gain a foothold in the Balkans, and at the end of the 14th c. Serbia and Greece were conquered. Constantinople was encircled, but owing to renewed attacks from the east by the Mongols it was another 50 years before the city was finally taken. In 1453 Constantinople became the capital of the Ottoman Empire and was renamed Istanbul (although internationally it continued to be known as Constantinople until 1923). The Byzantine Empire was at an end.

During the following centuries the Ottomans extended their dominions to include large areas of western Asia and North Africa and almost the whole of the Balkans. The empire reached the zenith of its power during the reign of Suleiman the Magnificent (1522–1566). He led the Turkish advance to the gates of Vienna but failed to take the city. From then on there followed a period of military stagnation and the Ottoman Empire also began to fall behind the European powers in economic and technical development. A second attack on Vienna in 1683 was again repulsed and the greater part of Hungary and Croatia was lost.

The Sick Man of the Bosporus

With the defeat at Vienna began the steady decline which transformed the mighty

Above: Atatürk
Right: Hadrian's Arch, Ephesus

Ottoman Empire into the 'sick man' of the Bosporus. The European powers used it as a pawn in their political manoeuverings, and though it survived for another 200 years, the empire grew steadily smaller. England, France, Austria and, above all, Russia harboured ambitions for Ottoman territory, while at the same time each feared the potential power which control would give to rival states. Since the time of Peter the Great, Russia had sought access to the Mediterranean through the Black Sea and had lent support to the independence movements in the Balkans. Time and again however the Russians found the other powers ready to come to the aid of the 'sick man' of Europe.

By the beginning of the First World War the Ottoman Empire had lost most of its possessions: regions bordering the Black Sea to Russia, Egypt to Britain, North Africa to France and Italy. The whole of the Balkans — as far as Thrace — was divided into independent states. After defeat in the First World War and after years of conflict with Greece, which was intent on regaining the former Greek enclaves in Anatolia, only the Turkish heartland in Asia Minor and European Thrace remained. The last Ottoman ruler was removed from office and the country became a republic.

The Republic of Turkey

The Ottoman Empire had not been able to isolate itself completely from the ideas of the European Enlightenment and the French Revolution. In the 19th c. a movement calling itself the 'Young Turks', whose motto was 'liberalism, reform and patriotism', gained in popularity, particularly in military circles among the officers. As a young man General Mustafa Kemal, Turkey's great reformer, later called Atatürk (Father of the Turks), had been a member of this movement. From his new capital Ankara, as the first president of modern Turkey, he brought in reforms to westernise the country. Turkey was declared a republic, state and religion were separated, and the sultanate and caliphate were abolished. After Atatürk's death in 1938 however there was repeated political unrest which resulted in intervention by the army.

For the Art lover

An artistic tradition specific to Turkey began only with the Scljuk art of the 11th c. A.D. and it shows little trace of influence by the cultures which flourished in

Topkapi Palace, interior of harem

Anatolia in earlier times. Only Imperial Byzantium provided any substantial cultural inheritance, primarily in the form of the many churches (especially in Istanbul) which were converted into mosques after the Muslim conquest. Most significantly as far as art was concerned the arrival of Islam led to the abandonment of figurative art, the pictorial representation of men and animals for religious purposes being prohibited by Islamic law. There are no large sculptures or religious wall paintings to be seen in any of Turkey's sacred buildings. The beauty of Turkish art lies much more in the exquisite detail of the ornamentation and the intricate development of its geometrical patterns and plant motifs. A multiplicity of designs woven together in delightful overall harmony is characteristic of the exceptionally fine ornamental wood, stone and stucco work which decorates the portals, windows, ceilings, prayer niches and stepped pulpits of Turkish mosques (there are some particularly beautiful examples to be seen in Konya). The same patterns and motifs, often making use of different shades of a single dominant colour, are found on the tiling which covers the walls of the mosques and also frequently the minarets.

At the end of the 13th and early in the 14th c. the Seljuks were ousted from their former position of power in Asia Minor by the Ottomans, a related Turkish people who carried on the main traditions of Islamic-Seljuk art. In the Ottoman period, however, a significant change took place in the architecture of mosques, the earlier pillared and multi-domed design giving way to buildings dominated by an increasingly prominent central dome. The influence of the Hagia Sophia Church in Constantinople in this development is unmistakable, with a central nave enclosed by colonnaded galleries becoming an established feature in Turkish mosques. The best examples of this new style of building can be seen in Bursa.

The most important architect of the Ottoman period was Mimar Sinan (born near Kayseri in 1489). He lived to be 99, and built more than 300 mosques, medreses, türbes, palaces, baths and bridges. His most famous buildings are the Suleiman Mosque in Istanbul, and the Selim Mosque in Edirne.

Under the Ottomans secular building also gained in importance, the most brilliant example being the Topkapi Serayi in Istanbul.

✄ Food and Drink

The Turks have the reputation of being the best cooks in the Near East, having cultivated the art of fine cooking since ancient times. Much of Turkish culinary tradition has however been lost: nowadays menus in the tourist hotels are 'international', and in the restaurants frequented by ordinary Turks the quality of the food varies enormously — as it does elsewhere of course. In many ways Turkish cooking is similar to Arab but in others it can be very distinctive. Strong spices are used only sparingly.

Yoghurt and pastries are both very popular, yoghurt also being used in sauces as well as with salads. A great variety of sweet pastries can be bought in the specialist dessert shops *(tatlicilar)*, while other shops *(börekciler* or *pastahane)* sell various savoury pies etc. *Muhallebici* are shops where milk-based dishes and soups can be obtained.

Lokanta is the Turkish word for an ordinary restaurant. Customers are quite often asked to go into the kitchen and choose their meal from the dishes being prepared. Then there are also *kebab* houses, which serve all kinds of kebab (grilled meat) and *köfte* (meat balls).

Coffee-houses in the country villages and in the smaller towns are patronised only by men. Sometimes, as in small hotels, they will serve a Turkish breakfast of bread, butter, jam, sheep's cheese, black olives and tea. Occasionally you may be offered *simits,* extremely tasty hard-baked rings sprinkled with sesame seeds, which are sold everywhere on the streets as well.

Desserts are almost always very sweet. The best known is *baklava,* slices of puff pastry filled with walnuts, pistachios and honey or cream.

Drinks

Many ordinary restaurants serve no alcohol, only fruit juices, which are often quite delicious, and *ayran,* a refreshing, thirst-quenching drink made from a mixture of yoghurt plus water, or lemonade. Mineral water *(maden suyu),* soda water *(soda)* and bottled spa water *(sise suyu)* are also generally available.

Better quality restaurants offer a wide selection of beer, wine and spirits. Good Turkish beers are *Tuborg* and *Efes* (light and dark beers or Pilsener). Wines range from a dry white wine, such as *Doluca extra dry* from the Sea of Marmara, to sweet wines and good strong red wines including *Buzbag* and *Kavaklidere.* Turkey is the world's sixth largest wine producer.

Baklava

Raki (distilled grape juice flavoured with aniseed) which should always be diluted with water, is drunk at any time, not just as an aperitif. In addition to Turkish brandy *(kanyak)* there is also a wonderfully colourful selection of liqueurs made from bananas, raspberries, peppermint etc., and of course, tea *(cay)* and coffee *(kahve).*

Hints for your holiday

. . . a cup of tea for the waiting visitor'

It's not just what you say . . .

Tact and politeness are the watchwords for the visitor to Turkey. The Turks are a sensitive people with a very strong sense of national pride, a pride easily aroused if they feel called upon to defend their fellow countrymen or their state. A good motto to remember is: 'It's not just what you say that matters, but how you say it'.

In Turkey as elsewhere officialdom and its ways can try the visitor's forbearance, and considerable patience therefore is required. Time in Anatolia goes at its own pace and administrative procedures can seem interminable, to Turks as well as to foreigners. Nevertheless they are generally conducted in a courteous atmosphere which will often include the offer of a cup of tea for the waiting visitor.

As a rule foreigners are treated as guests, particularly in country areas where custom and tradition are still strong. It is not uncommon to be invited spontaneously to take some refreshment — in a courtyard, in front of a house, or even in a field if a farmer happens to be having lunch — or to be drawn into local festivities. In places not yet reached by mass tourism it is important to remember not to offer money in return for hospitality; your Turkish hosts would feel deeply insulted. In tourist centres on the other hand, baksheesh is a magic formula which simplifies business and smooths over a host of problems.

Bargaining, *pazarlik,* is still commonplace in Turkey, amounting almost to a national pastime. The carpet seller in the bazaar expects customers to haggle over the price of his merchandise, though anyone who haggles for a longish time should also make the purchase in the end. In modern department stores goods must by law carry a label showing the cost to the retailer and the price at which they are being sold, and bargaining is frowned upon. On the souvenir stalls you can feel free to push the price down with a clear conscience, even if the stall-holder swears by Allah that he is losing money in the deal!

Sunset off Istanbul

Where to go and what to see

Thrace and Istanbul

All roads to Istanbul, jewel of European Turkey and gateway to Asia Minor, pass through Thrace. Approaching from the west the motorist has a choice between the E 5 via Sofia, crossing the Turkish frontier just before Edirne, or the E 55 from Thessalonika, crossing at Ipsala. Only those driving south from the Bulgarian Black Sea coastal resorts are likely to make use of the border crossing at Malko Tarnovo/Aziziye. Turkish Thrace is part of what was once the ancient province of Macedonia, most of which now lies in northern Greece and southern Bulgaria. Travelling through the region the contrast between the three areas immediately catches the eye: the mountains of Thrace are less high and craggy than those of Greek Macedonia and the land is altogether less fertile than the Bulgarian plain. Parts of Thrace consist of treeless steppe, similar to the distinctive landscape of much of Anatolia, but there are also forest-covered highlands running with game, especially in the Istranca range bordering the Black Sea where the mountains reach a height of 1031 m. The flood plain of the river Maritza (Meriç in Turkish) which forms the frontier with Greece is part marshland, part fertile alluvium. There are fields of tobacco, maize, wheat and barley, vineyards and orchards, and flocks of brown, white and black sheep reared for their wool.

For the traveller from Europe entering Thrace the transition from West to East is very marked, particularly in the buildings and the people. Bazaars and mosques are a feature of even the smaller towns, and the sight of women in traditional Turkish costume, with wide, colourful trousers and headscarves, becomes a common one. Menus, the attitude to time, and all too frequently the lack of hygiene, are also distinctly oriental.

Among the cities of Thrace only Edirne and Istanbul boast truly outstanding monuments to a brilliant cultural past; but many others possess 15th and 16th c. mosques, caravanserais, fountains, bridges and *bedestes* (covered bazaars) by the great Ottoman architects Hayreddin and, above all, Sinan. For instance, in Babaeski and Lüleburgaz between Edirne and Istanbul there are mosques designed by Sinan, and there is a picturesque, typically eastern market in the small port of Tekirdag on the Sea of Marmara. In the north-east near Corlu there are ruins of a beautiful Roman bridge.

Edirne Alt. 41 m; Pop. 150,000

Edirne is the provincial capital of one of four provinces in European Turkey. It is also the most important town on the main route from central Europe to Istanbul and stands at the confluence of the rivers Meriç and Tunca.

 The former Adrianople

The town was first established by the Roman Emperor Hadrian in A.D. 125 and was originally named Hadrianopolis — or Adrianople — after its founder. From the 4th c. onwards it grew rapidly, controlled at various times by the Goths, Avars, Bulgars and Crusaders. In 1361 it was captured by the Ottoman Sultan Murat I who made it his capital and changed the name to Edirne. Fate has not always treated Edirne kindly. From time to time parts of the town have been destroyed by earthquakes and fires and in later centuries, as in earlier, it has found itself in various different hands. In 1829 it was occupied by the Russians, in 1854 by the French; in 1877 the Russians returned, and from 1881 to 1922 it was under the control of Greece. Today Edirne is a typical provincial capital.

 Famous Mosques

The Selim Mosque is Edirne's outstanding attraction with its four slender minarets rising above the roofs of the town, each being 80 m high with three balconies. It takes its name from the Sultan Selim II whose ambition was to give the city a building of incomparable beauty. This ambition was realised through the genius of the architect Sinan, whose life's work was crowned, at the age of 90, by the construction of this mosque. The interior, bathed in light, is roofed over by a great dome — larger even than the dome of the Hagia Sophia in Istanbul — supported by four massive porphyry columns and four pillars. The *mimber* (pulpit) is finely decorated with tiles. The Seljuk portal was once part of a mosque near Izmir, and in the forecourt some of the 16 columns ingeniously incorporated into the arcades came originally from the Dionysos Theatre in Athens. The former *medrese* (Koranic school) attached to the mosque now houses a small museum of archaeology and folklore containing finds from archaeological digs, and Ottoman gravestones.

The Beyazit Camii with its two minarets is made all the more impressive by the unspoiled beauty of its setting on the banks of the Tunca. Designed by Hayreddin between 1484 and 1488 it is a large square stone building, devoid of pillars and arches, topped by a single mighty dome. Among the buildings attached to the mosque, the former lunatic asylum, its spacious rooms embellished with niches and fountains, has a particularly interesting history.

Here attempts were made as early as the 15th and 16th centuries to treat the mentally ill with music and occupational therapy. Although not officially open to visitors its iron gate is never shut. Sadly both the asylum and the former Koranic school are now somewhat neglected.

Other buildings of note are the Uc Serefeli Mosque with its many domes and pillars, the Murat Mosque beautifully decorated with tiles, the Eski Cami (Old Mosque), the 12th c. Clock Tower (restored in the 19th c.), once part of the town fortifications, and the 15th and 16th c. bridges.

At the end of May or in the first half of June a wrestling tournament is held on *Sarayliçi Island*, part of a tradition going back to the 14th c. With their chests and arms smeared with oil and wearing long black leather trousers, the 'strongmen' of the region do battle with one another.

The *Ali Pasa Bazaar* sells everything from a leg of mutton to valuable gold jewellery. Prices are usually more reasonable than in Istanbul or Izmir since Edirne is not so inundated with tourists.

Turkish baths. There are several baths *(hamam)* in Edirne. The *Çifte Hamam* in Üç Serefeli Square was designed by the architect Sinan in the 16th c.

In the Hotel *Sultan* and the *Rüstempasa Hani* (a 16th c. caravanserai).

In the hotels.

Plenty of choice, especially in the bazaar quarter.

BP Mocamp Aycekadin on the outskirts of town on the Istanbul road, and *Camping Meric* on the banks of the Maritza.

Grease wrestling, Edirne

Istanbul Pop. 6 million

Only the Bosporus separates Beyoglu from Üsküdar, just 700 m separating Europe and Asia! Beyoglu to the west and Üsküdar to the east are both districts of Istanbul, the only city in the world to straddle two continents. Istanbul's unique location greatly contributes to its special atmosphere and fascination, captured in any number of famous films and novels.

From the Sea of Marmara the city extends to encircle the southern end of the Bosporus and its tributary the Golden Horn, by far the greater part lying on the European side. Like Rome, Istanbul is built on seven hills, and the city is divided into three districts: Stanbul, the old town, built between the Sea of Marmara and the Golden Horn on the remains of old Byzantium; Beyoğlu, the modern city, north of the Golden Horn; and, across the Bosporus in Asia, Üsküdar (formerly Scutari) with Kadiköy.

Many rulers, many names

Some three thousand years ago the site of present-day Istanbul was occupied by a Thracian settlement, Lygos. Then around 660 B.C. the Dorians established themselves, calling their settlement Byzantion after their leader Byzas. Following the Roman occupation the town was renamed Augusta Antoninia. Later, when Constantine the Great made it his

capital, the name was changed yet again to Nova Roma, but it soon became known as Constantinopolis. Constantinople was for centuries the capital of the eastern Roman, later the Byzantine, Empire, falling eventually to the onslaught of the Ottoman Turks. The Turks under Mehmet II occupied the city on May 29th 1453, after which it became their metropolis and was renamed Istanbul. It continued as the capital of Turkey until 1923 and remains the country's largest city and its cultural and economic centre.

Impressions of Istanbul

Istanbul today still has the aura of a city in an eastern fairy-tale. At night hundreds of coloured lights are reflected in the dark waters of the Bosporus and the Golden Horn while others, shining out from innumerable windows and street lamps, appear to climb the surrounding hills. Flood-lit minarets pierce the purple night sky and, even as the muezzin calls the

faithful to the last prayers of the day, the first sounds of drum and flute issuing their invitation to the belly dance are already adrift on the evening air.

In bright daylight the city is no less evocative, its golden domes gleaming in the brilliant sunshine. Street vendors selling honey and fatty pastries call their wares, and nimble shoe-shine boys fall upon dusty feet with bits of rag, water, spit and a variety of smelly concoctions. Amid the indescribably chaotic tangle of motor-traffic a donkey trots by, apparently quite without concern. In the bazaars every conceivable spice from the orient celebrates its presence in an orgy of smells, while men bend almost double under the weight of loads much bigger than themselves. In the mosque an old man reads his *surahs* from the Koran unperturbed by the tourists, and next to it fishermen offer their glistening and still struggling catch for sale from boats packed with sheep, goats and chickens. In the Old Town, in small cafés that have escaped the tourist invasion, men sip their Turkish coffee, as they have done since long, long ago.

📷 Sightseeing in old Istanbul

Every visitor to Istanbul should take one of the organised bus tours round the major sights. Although Istanbul is mainly in Europe it is also an exotic eastern city teeming with ill-informed, self-appointed guides on the look-out for tips (baksheesh), with a local populace who are helpful but speak only Turkish, with a bewildering maze of narrow streets and alleys, and served by taxi drivers greedy for fares.

The Topkapi Seraglio (Topkapi Serayi: Canon Gate Palace), a very large complex of palace buildings, is an undisputed architectural masterpiece. Construction was begun in 1462 by Mehmet II, the walled palace later being enlarged by Suleiman I (1522–1566). It remained the official residence of the Ottoman sultans until 1855 when the Dolmabahçe Palace took its place.

The Topkapi Seraglio houses many treasures, including a magnificent collection of porcelain formerly belonging to the sultans and the harem, on display in the palace kitchens on the right-hand side of the main court.

The third court, the inner precinct of the palace, is reached through the Bab-i-Saadat (Gate of Felicity). Of special interest are the Audience Hall, Ahmet III's Library, built in 1719 entirely of marble and containing 4000 valuable Greek, Persian, Arabic and Turkish manuscripts, and the Treasury of the Ottoman rulers. The most spectacular single item is undoubtedly the throne of Shah Ismail.

A passage next to the portrait gallery leads through to a fourth courtyard where there is a terrace overlooking the Sea of Marmara. As well as a restaurant there are several other pavilions. The most splendid of these is the Baghdad Pavilion *(Bağdad Köşkü)*; from a small balcony covered by a bronze canopy there is another superb view. Turning left from this vantage point leads the visitor through the Circumcision Room into two beautifully decorated rooms containing sacred relics and other objects. Not on any account to be missed, these include hair from the prophet Mohammed's beard, and his footprint, as well as his mantle, sword, and standard.

Of all the rooms to be visited, the harem, a self-contained series of apartments, is most charged with the atmosphere of the orient.

The whole Topkapi complex is open every day except Tuesday from 9.30 a.m. to 5 p.m.

Tiles in the harem, Topkapi Palace

The Hagia Sophia

The Hagia Sophia (Aya Sofya) is the most famous building in Turkey. From the outside it is not particularly impressive, many additions to the structure and a hotchpotch of surrounding buildings having marred the exterior. Constantine the Great founded the first Church of the Divine Wisdom (in Greek, Hagia Sophia) on the site in 326. This church burned down in 404, and though by 415 it had been rebuilt, it was again destroyed by fire in 532. Only 39 days later the Emperor Justinian laid the foundation stone of the present building. The church was consecrated anew in 562, and again in 994 after having been damaged in an earthquake.

On May 29th 1453 the Ottoman army led by Mehmet II occupied Istanbul. The church was immediately converted into a mosque and within two days of its capture the Sultan took part in Friday prayers there. The Turks built minarets, fountains, a kitchen, mausoleums (*türbes*) and other additions but made virtually no alterations to the main building. Only the magnificent mosaics disappeared under a layer of plaster, in accordance with Islamic doctrine which prohibits figural art in holy places. Work began on exposing and restoring the mosaics in 1931 when, on Atatürk's instructions, the mosque became a museum.

Entrance is through the Theodosius vestibule which leads into the narthex, the vestibule of the old Christian basilica. Above the central doorway is a superb 10th c. gold mosaic.

The Hagia Sophia is the fourth largest church in the world after St Peter's in Rome and the great cathedrals of Seville and Milan. The massive nave roofed by the huge dome is still considered an architectural wonder. The nave is dominated by its not quite circular dome, 55.6 m high with diameters of 30.8 m and 31.9 m, encircled by a ring of 40 windows. Of special interest are the fine 16th c. marble pulpit and the Omphalos — the Navel of the World — a mosaic floor inlaid with rare stones on which the Byzantine emperors were crowned.

The exit is through bronze doors dating from the 9th c. The Hagia Sophia is open every day except Monday from 9.30 a.m. to 5 p.m.

Behind the Hagia Sophia some of Old Istanbul's terrace houses have been restored.

The Yerebatan Cistern was constructed by the Emperor Justinian in the 6th century. The palace-like underground cistern was built to safeguard the water supply in times of crisis. The vaulted brick roof of the 140 m-long and 73 m-wide reservoir is supported by 336 columns, some with Corinthian capitals.

Horse Square (At Meydani), the former Roman Hippodrome, and the Blue Mosque, are separated from the Hagia Sophia by a small park.

In the square there are two obelisks. The first, the Egyptian obelisk (Dikilitaş), cut from a single piece of porphyry, came from the temple at Karnak (14th c. B.C.). It was erected in the Hippodrome in A.D. 390 by the Emperor Theodosius. The second, the Mortar-Built Column (Örme Sütun), was probably stripped of its gilded facing panels at the time of the Crusades.

The 5th c. B.C. Snake Column is the oldest Greek monument in the city. It was erected at Delphi in 479 B.C. to commemorate the victory over the Persian army at Plataeae.

The Blue Mosque or Sultan Ahmet Mosque (Sultanahmet Camii) is now the city's main mosque. Built between 1609 and 1616 it is the only mosque in the world to have six minarets. The exterior is the most beautiful in the city, and the interior excelled only by that of the Hagia Sophia. Four huge columns support the dome which is decorated with painted ornamentation, predominantly in blue but with some green also, and including calligraphic inscriptions of the names of the caliphs. The tiling on the walls, again in shades

The Blue Mosque

of blue and green, contrasts pleasingly with the red prayer rugs. The white marble pulpit is a copy of the pulpit at Mecca.

The Bazaar (Kapali Çarşi) is the world's largest. Built of wood in 1461 the original Old Market grew over the centuries into the bazaar. Destroyed several times by fire it acquired its present appearance in 1954. In the labyrinth of half-lit, mostly vaulted alleys covering more than 200,000 sq. m, there is an astonishing selection of goods to be seen, ranging from junk such as rusty knives to gold jewellery.

The Beyazit Camii (1498–1505) just north of the bazaar is definitely worth a visit. The 24-domed building, designed by the architect Hayreddin, was the first large mosque to be constructed following the occupation of Constantinople by the Turks.

The Suleiman Mosque (Süleymaniye Camii) has four minarets, all of different heights, and exquisite stained-glass windows and tiling. It was built between 1550 and 1557 for Suleiman the Magnifi-

The Suleiman Mosque

cent by the outstanding Ottoman architect Sinan. The mosque and its numerous subsidiary buildings, including schools, baths and libraries, now form almost a separate locality on their own.

The Rüstem Paşa Mosque (Rüstem Paşa Camii) has an interior most beautifully decorated with Iznik tiles.

The New Mosque (Yeni Cami) by the Galata Bridge dates from the early 18th c. The gilded stalactites in the prayer room make it well worth a visit.

The Land Walls, built during the Byzantine period to protect the imperial capital against attack by land, extend for nearly 7 km from the Sea of Marmara to the Golden Horn. They are an impressive sight, both the inner and the outer walls being fortified with 96 towers.

The Fortress of Yedicule stands at the western end of the Land Walls, by the Sea of Marmara. It is now a museum (closed on Monday).

The Church of St Saviour in Chora (Kariye Camii) was converted into a mosque around 1500 but is now a museum. The superb 14th c. frescoes and mosaics of scenes from the New Testament were uncovered and painstakingly restored between 1947 and 1951. There is a small tea garden next to the church.

Mosque of the Conquest (Fethiye Camii), a little way towards the city centre from the Church of St Saviour, was once a monastery. From the outside it is still very much a Byzantine basilica while inside there are some very fine mosaics decorating the dome.

📷 Golden Horn and Beyoğlu

Modern Istanbul, Beyoğlu, lies opposite the old town of Stanbul, separated from it by the Golden Horn but linked to it by the Galata and Atatürk bridges. The Galata Bridge rests on 22 pontoons and, thronged with colourful crowds, is a popular setting for photographs.

The Dolmabahçe Palace on the Bosporus, built in 1853 in the opulent style of the Turkish neo-Renaissance, is the only major building of historical interest in the new town. It was formerly the imperial palace and for a short time after 1877 housed the state parliament. Following extensive restoration the palace is once again open to the public (9.30 a.m.–5 p.m., except Monday and Thursday and during State receptions). Among more than 200 rooms the most interesting are the Throne Room and the room in which Atatürk died.

The Galata Tower is also of historic interest, the lower part with its 3 m-thick walls dating back to the 6th c. The tower now houses nightclubs and speciality restaurants.

The Nusreti Mosque (1873) is an attractive blend of Baroque and traditional architectural styles. In

Kariye Camii (the Church of St Saviour)

Tophane Square nearby there is a beautiful 18th c. marble fountain.

Taksim Square is the centre of Beyoğlu. The Independence Monument commemorates Atatürk's decisive battle against the Greeks and the declaration of the Republic.

 ## Old buildings, new life

Among the old buildings once in a state of disrepair but now carefully restored and given new life are:

The Konak Centre between the Hagia Sophia and the Blue Mosque was formerly an old wooden palace and other buildings. The Konak Hotel with its old carpets, old-fashioned brass bedsteads and gas lamps etc. recaptures the atmosphere of times gone by. Next to it is a handicrafts market (formerly an 18th c. Koranic school) with workshops and a tea-garden in the courtyard.

The Yildiz Park Pavilions in the spacious park between the Dolmabahçe Palace and Europa Bridge, are delightful places to enjoy morning coffee or tea. The Malta Pavilion and the Çadir Pavilion, both now cafés, are furnished in the style of the 19th c. Decorated entirely in pink and white the Pink Serra is a tea-room and pastry shop, and also has a display of antique wineglasses.

The Emirgan Park Pavilions. In Emirgan Park, behind the Rumeli Hisari on the shores of the Bosporus, there are cafés in the Yellow Pavilion and in the Pink Pavilion (which also houses a small museum of the Bosporus). Concerts are held in the White or 'Music' Pavilion.

Büyük Çamlica on the Asiatic side of the Bosporus is the highest point in Istanbul and commands some wonderful views. Three Ottoman-style coffee-houses have been built on Camlica Hill.

 ## Europa Bridge and Üsküdar

Across the Bosporus, Üsküdar, with its picturesque old wooden houses and

Interior of Dolmabahçe Palace

narrow alleys, retains more of an oriental character than Stambul.

Üsküdar can be reached either by the Kabataş car ferry, by steamer from the Galata Bridge or over the Bosporus (Europa) Bridge, opened in 1973 as part of Istanbul's 22 km orbital road. It is the first bridge in the world to link two continents; with a length of 1560 m and spanning 1074 m it was, at the time of building, Europe's longest suspension bridge.

At the Asiatic end of the Bosporus bridge is the former Beylerbeyi Palace (1865) notable for its lavish interior décor (closed on Monday and Thursday).

🏛 A museum journey through four thousand years

Istanbul has some very important museum collections (entrance fees vary from about 25 pence to £1).

Details about opening hours can be obtained at the Information Office in Sultan Ahmet Square.

The Archaeological Museum (Arkeoloji Müzesi; open daily except Monday, 9.30 a.m.–5 p.m.) near the Topkapi Palace, contains some outstanding art-treasures. Especially worth seeing are the Satraps' Sarcophagus (5th c. B.C.), the Alexander Sarcophagus (4th c. B.C.), the Sarcophagus of the Mourning Women (about 350 B.C.) and the impressive remains of the temple friezes from Magnesia and Lagina.

The Museum of the Ancient Orient (Şark Eserleri Müzesi; open daily except Monday, 9.30 a.m.–5 p.m.) next to the Archaeological Museum houses the major archaeological finds from the former Ottoman territories. Nearly every early archaeological period is represented.

The Museum of Turkish and Islamic Art (Türk ve Islâm Eserleri Müzesi; open daily except Monday, 10 a.m.–5 p.m.) in the Ibrahim Pasa Palace next to the Blue Mosque, has some unique early copies of the Koran as well as collections of miniatures, carpets and prayer rugs, textiles, ceramics, carvings and sculpture.

The Tile Museum (Çinili Kösk, open daily except Monday and Thursday, 9.30 a.m.–5 p.m.) is immediately opposite the Archaeological Museum.

The Military Museum (Askeri Müzesi; open daily except Monday and Tuesday, 9 a.m.–12 noon and 1 p.m.–5 p.m.) is located behind the Hilton Hotel. On display are uniforms and weaponry from the Ottoman Empire including military costumes and armour belonging to the Sultans. From time to time the Band of the Janissaries plays at the museum, dressed in their traditional uniform.

The main shopping area in Beyoğlu is around Taksim Square, along Istiklal Caddesi and Cumhuriyet Caddesi in particular.

Men in search of an evening's entertainment in Istanbul tend to think only of belly dancing, but anyone who expects the performances to match those of Moroccan or Egyptian dancers will be disappointed. Except for hotels and international nightclubs, the city's bars and night spots are not normally frequented by women.

Istanbul is an international art and cultural centre offering a wide selection of opera, concerts, folk music, folk dancing and discothèques. The dearest seats at the opera cost about £4.

The restaurant in the Galata Tower serves international and Turkish dishes. It is not cheap but it has a lovely view.

In Stambul: *Pandeli* in the Egyptian bazaar (only open at lunchtime); *Konya Lezzet Lokantasi* on Ankara Cad.; *Topkapi Sarayi Lokantasi* in the Topkapi Palace. — In Beyoğlu: *Bap Kafeterya,* Yeşilçam Sok.; *Haci Salih Lokantasi,* Sakizagaci Sok. — In Karaköy: *Liman Lokantasi,* Rihtim Cad.

The Istanbul international arts festival is held in June and July and includes theatre, concerts, folk music and folk dancing, mostly in open-air historic settings such as the Rumeli Hiseri.

During the summer season *son et lumière* performances are given in front of the Sultan Ahmed Mosque, bringing to life events in Istanbul's history (English commentaries).
There is a drama festival at the end of September.

Republic Day (October 29th) is celebrated with processions and other events.

Turkish baths (hamam), including the *Cağaloğlu Hamami* (near the Blue Mosque) and the *Galatasaray Hamami.*

Taxis are fitted with meters. Check that they are properly set (at 'Gün' during the day and at 'Gece' - with a 50% surcharge - at night).

Buses are a reasonably priced, convenient form of transport for anyone sufficiently familiar with the city (tickets for the red buses are bought from the street sellers, those for the blue buses from the conductor). In Istanbul itself the municipal authority also runs a system of shared taxis (*dolmuş*) with fixed pick-up points.

In Bakirköy (on the E 5) and in Yesilyurt (near the airport).

There are information bureaux at the airport, in the harbour building and in the Hilton Hotel. The municipal information office is in the kiosk in Sultan Ahmet Square.

Left: Europa Bridge, Istanbul. Above: Rumeli Hisari

Bosporus, Sea of Marmara and the Dardanelles

The Bosporus, the Sea of Marmara and the Dardanelles divide Turkey into its European and Asiatic parts.

The Bosporus (Boğaziçi), 32 km long, links the Sea of Marmara and the Black Sea, varying in width from only 660 m at Rumeli Hisari, the narrowest point, to almost 3.3 km at Büyükdere. Much the best way of being introduced to the fascinating scenery, culture and history of the Bosporus is to take a boat trip, or one of the combined excursions by boat and bus.

The Sea of Marmara (Marmara Denizi) is 280 km long, up to 80 km wide and over 1000 m deep. It has two groups of islands, the Princes' Islands south-east of Istanbul and the four Marmara Islands near Erdek.

The Dardanelles, 65 km long, are bounded on the European side by the Gallipoli peninsula. At Çannakkale, the narrowest point, they are 1.3 km wide.

The Bosporus

Although the water is clearer than in many places on the Sea of Marmara, the Bosporus resorts are not recommended for anyone wanting to swim. There are numerous, dangerous eddies and the waterside hotels and bathing places have only wooden staging or concrete terraces.

The ferries across the Bosporus and the boats which make the daily excursions leave from the Galata Bridge in Istanbul. With stops on both the European and Asiatic sides the round trip excursion takes about 7 hours.

Beşiktaş with its monument to one of Suleiman I's admirals Hayreddin Paşa (16th c.) is first in view on the left bank after leaving Istanbul, soon followed by Ortaköy with its neo-Renaissance mosque (1854). To the right on the Asiatic side are Beylerbeyi and the small town of Çengelköy. The Rococo palace at Beylerbeyi was built by Abdul Aziz in 1865.

Between Ortaköy and Beylerbeyi

Black Sea

Sea of Marmara

Bosporus

Princes' Islands

5 km

shipping passes under the Europa Bridge (see page 27). Along both waterfronts are wooden villas or *yalis* built originally by rich Istanbul merchants and dignitories; some of the villas have been beautifully restored.

Next in view on the left bank, nestling against the side of a hill, is the small town of Arnavutköy, a former Albanian settlement well worth visiting for its narrow streets and picturesque little wooden houses; further along still is Bebek with its pretty restaurants, a popular place for outings. On the right is Vaniköy, and then Kandilli, site of the Abdülmecit Palace.

The straits between the two fortresses of Rumeli Hisari (left) and Anadolu Hisari (right) provide the most striking and photogenic scenery of the entire trip up the Bosporus. The magnificently preserved Rumeli Hisari (European Fortress) has an imposing bastion, crenellated walls and three mighty towers, the round east tower being 22 m in diameter. It was built by the Sultan Mehmet II in 1452 during

the siege of Constantinople, taking only 96 days to erect. The smaller Anadolu Hisari (Anatolian Fortress) was constructed earlier, in the 14th c. (Both fortresses are open to the public.) It was here at the narrows that the Persian king Darius I built a bridge of boats over the Bosporus in 514 B.C., crossing with his army of 500,000 men.

On the left beyond the narrows is Emirgân (another favourite place for outings), followed by Istinyie with its shipyard (in a bay), and Yeniköy with its beautiful villas and vineyards. In succession on the opposite bank are Kanlica, famous for its yoghourt and little waterside restaurants, Çubuklu where there is a residence built by one of the Egyptian Khedives, Paşabahçe with its ruined 16th c. palace belonging to the Sultan Murat III, and Beykoz, at the northern end of Beykoz Bay.

Next on the European side in a small bay beyond Yeniköy is Tarabya with its restaurants, hotel, marina and military cemetery, and further on, following close one upon another, Büyükdere, Sariyer — which has some good fish restaurants and a famous pie shop — and Yenimahalle, a fishing village with a small 18th c. fortress (confronted on the Asiatic shore by Yuşa fort).

At the north end of the Bosporus is a military zone where landing is prohibited, the last ports of call for the excursion boats being Rumeli Kavagi on the left bank with its 17th c. fort nearby, and Anadolu Kavagi on the right bank, in Macar Bay. A ruined Byzantine castle can be seen on the northern promontory of the bay. Flanking the Bosporus where it enters the Black Sea are two lighthouses, Rumeli Feneri and Anadolu Feneri.

The Princes' Islands

The nine Princes' Islands lie off the Asiatic shore of the Sea of Marmara about 10 km south of Istanbul. Only the four largest, ranging from 1.3 to 5.4 sq.

km, are of real interest to the tourist. A ferry service to the islands runs several times a day from the Galata Bridge in Istanbul, taking between 1 and 2 hours. The name 'Princes' Islands' dates from the time of the east Roman-Byzantine Empire when princes and other members of the imperial family were frequently confined there, sometimes for their own protection. The ruins of churches and monasteries built during the period can still be seen. The Turkish name for the islands is Kizil Adalar (Red Islands) because of the rust coloured soil.

The inhabitants of the four islands at which the boat calls, Kinali, Burgaz, Heybeli and Büyük, number some 25,000 in all, but with the many holiday homes belonging to people from Istanbul the population in summer swells to over 150,000. To these are added the many day-trippers who come to bathe, picnic and take the island air. The islands retain something of a turn-of-the-century atmosphere, particularly because they are free of motor traffic, transport being by horse-drawn, canopied buggies costing between £3 and £6 for a round trip. The red colour of the soil is most pronounced on the smallest island Kinali Ada while on the slightly larger neighbouring island of Burgaz Ada a 165 m hill offers a fine panoramic view over the whole island group. In Classical times there were copper mines on Heybeli Ada (which has a beautiful bathing beach). One of the three monasteries on Heybeli Ada has been rebuilt and its iconostasis is well worth walking up the hill to see. Cadets are still trained at the naval academy founded by the Ottoman Sultans in 1793.

Büyük Ada, the largest and most popular of the islands, has lush vegetation and a number of pleasant restaurants and tea-rooms. A climb to its ruined monastery is rewarded by the distant view from the top of Yücetepe, the island's 200 m hill.

Sea of Marmara

On the coast near Istanbul there are several seaside resorts popular with local people and very crowded on summer weekends. Ataköy, Yeşilköy and Florya are the best known, with the nicest beaches.

Elsewhere on the Sea of Marmara the resorts also cater mainly for Turkish holidaymakers. Set among pine trees and olive groves Erdek with its long, partly sandy, partly rocky beaches, is usually crowded with people. There are ferries from Erdek to the islands of Marmara, Avşar and Pasalimani.

The two little ports of Mudanya and Yalova on the south-east coast are really of interest only because they lie en route to the historic towns of Bursa and Iznik, though Yalova is popular with the Turks and Arabs as a spa town with good treatment facilities and thermal baths.

Bursa Alt. 225 m; Pop. 500,000

Narrow winding streets, picturesque old houses, splendid mosques, a densely populated bazaar quarter filled with the smells of the orient, bridges spanning deep ravines in the middle of town, old tombs in romantic, cypress-shaded gardens alongside wide modern boulevards, famous thermal springs, hotels, restaurants, and thriving industries — Bursa has all of these and more. With the mighty Ulu Dağ massif (2543 m) for a backcloth it is one of the most beautiful cities in Turkey.

The First Capital of the Ottoman Empire

Bursa, in common with almost every city in the Ottoman Empire, has had a chequered history. It owed its birth originally to Hannibal on whose advice King Prusias I of Bithynia founded the city in 186 B.C., and achieved considerable importance under the Romans, during whose period of

Bursa

domination palaces, baths and indoor markets were built. The Roman governor of Bithynia, Pliny, also established a large library in the town. This rich Roman legacy was inherited by the Byzantines who in turn were forced to yield it to the young Ottoman prince Orhan, son of Osman I, in 1326.

Bursa became the first capital of the Ottoman Empire, which it remained until 1361 when Edirne was captured. Following their victory at Ankara in 1402 the city was sacked by Tamarlane's Mongols, quickly recovering however from the destruction. In the 19th c. the town was badly damaged by fire and earthquake. Today it is one of Turkey's major industrial centres manufacturing cars and textiles etc., despite which it retains its charm and beauty.

Mosques and Mausoleums

The Great Mosque (Ulu Cami) is the most important building in the city. Started in 1379 under Murat I and completed in 1421 under Mehmet I it is the earliest example of a multi-pillared mosque, its 12 pillars supporting 19 flattened domes adorned with calligraphic inscriptions of quotations from the Koran. In the centre of the prayer hall is a fountain. Of special interest are the exceptionally fine

Mausoleum of Mehmet I, Bursa

cedarwood pulpit (made in 1400) and the prayer niche decorated with blue, gold, red and black tiles.

From **Citadel Hill** there is a magnificent panoramic view over the city. Only a few remnants of wall have survived from the original defences. The mausoleums of Osman I and Orhan, the first Ottoman rulers, date only from the 19th c., the originals having been destroyed in an earthquake.

The Green Mosque (Yeşil Cami) in the eastern part of the city is the finest mosque in Bursa, built in 1421 by the Sultan Mehmet. Although undistinguished from the outside (the tiles having fallen off the minarets during the 1855 earthquake) the interior is quite superb. The prayer hall, divided into two chambers, is almost completely lined with exceptionally lovely green and blue tiles. The wooden door and window frames are decorated with *surahs* from the Koran and elaborately carved marble work embellishes the windows.

The Green Medrese next to the Green Mosque houses the Museum of Turkish and Islamic Art (art and artefacts of the Ottoman period) which should certainly be visited.

Across the road from the mosque stands the Yeşil Türbe (1419), the mausoleum of Mehmet I. At the head of the sarcophagus rests a large white silk turban, symbol of the Sultan's high rank.

The Yildirim Camii (also called the Beyazit Mosque), built in the 14th c. and once magnificent, was almost totally destroyed in the 1855 earthquake and much altered during restoration. It is still worth seeing for the ornamented marble portal which has survived. A short distance below the mosque is the mausoleum of Beyazit I.

The Türbes in the garden of the mosque are also worth seeing, the cemetery with its ancient plantains and cypresses being one of the most fascinating in Turkey. Among the 15th and 16th c. tombs the mausoleum of

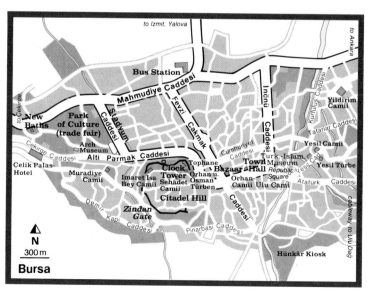

Bursa

Murat II is most unusual. The architect designed the tomb with a dome which is open at the top, fulfilling the Sultan's final wish for 'the rain to water my grave and the singing of the birds to reach me there'. The conical dome of Princess Devletşah Hatun's mausoleum is also unique, while the tomb of Princess Şehzade is made special by its exceptionally beautiful tiles. Opposite the cemetery, the Muradiye Camii, a splendidly colourful, half-timbered 17th c. building, is open to the public and also merits a visit.

The Archaeological Museum (containing important art treasures from the Greek, Roman and Byzantine periods and a fine collection of coins) is located in the Culture Park.

Çekirge. For anyone interested in art and architecture a visit to Bursa would not be complete without taking the 3 km bus or taxi ride to the suburb of Çekirge. Here there is a 14th c. bath (Eski Kaplica), still in use, its windowless domes creating the appearance of a fortress. Next to it is the Murat I Mosque, the oldest in Bursa, built in 1365. The arches in the façade show the influence of Italian architecture. In the mausoleum opposite are the remains of the Sultan Murat I who, before the battle of Kosova in 1389, was stabbed to death by the Serbian general Miloš Obilić.

  From Istanbul to Bursa (230 km) via Izmit, Yalova and Gemlik.

  From Istanbul-Kabataş to Yalova; then by bus or dolmus to Bursa (50 km).

H The Roman emperors bathed in Bursa's thermal springs. As well as the old baths in Çekirge there are several others opposite the Hotel Çelik Palas. Some hotels also have their own.

 It is easy enough to enjoy oneself in Bursa, there being a good selection of bars, discothèques and night-clubs which offer everything from belly dancing and Turkish folk music and dance to (rather mediocre) floor shows. There are several cinemas which show American, European and other films. A walk through the Culture Park can also be highly recommended.

  In July (the exact date varies from year to year) there is a festival at which the famous Bursa sword dancers perform.

  Hotel *Çelik Palas*.

  Turkish specialities in the Iskender Lakantasi, and in the restaurants in Atatürk Caddesi.

  The bazaar quarter is to the north of the Great Mosque. Even those with no desire to buy will enjoy wandering through the covered bazaar (*bedesten*) while nobody looking for a souvenir of Bursa can fail to find something to their taste, whether it be a hand-knotted carpet, some 'antique' — guaranteed reproduction! — or a Turkish 'hubble-bubble' pipe.

A BP *Kumluk Mocamp* (with swimming pool) 6 km from Bursa on the road to Yalova.

Ulu Dağ Alt. 2543 m
The only high mountains in the Marmara area are in the Ulu Dağ massif, Ulu Dağ being the name also of the highest peak and of the small hotel complex (1800 m). At the time of the Bithynian kingdom the massif was believed to be an Olympus, abode of the gods. In later times brigands and monks lived here. Today it is the most popular year-round resort in north-west Anatolia.

By cable car from Bursa, 30 minutes to the peak; or by car, also 30 minutes from Bursa, driving first to Soğukpinar and then turning left up a steep mountain road as far as the resort.

From the resort to the various peaks (between 1917 m and 2543 m high) in two or three hours; ridge walks starting from the cable car station at the summit.

 In streams full of trout.

 Swimming pool at the Hotel *Panorama Oberj.*

 Several chair- and ski-lifts in the vicinity of the peaks. Beautiful, almost treeless ski country. Ski season from the end of November to the beginning of April. Also international ski events. Skating at the hotel complex.

 At the Hotel *Panorama Oberj.*

 Additional excursions to the small port of Yalova (56 km), and to the bird sanctuary at Lake Manyas (73 km) where 23 different species nest, including some very rare ones.

Iznik Alt. 57 m; Pop. 12,000

Iznik lies on a large lake of the same name, about 60 km from Bursa and the same distance from Yalova.

 The City of Tile Makers

Iznik, the ancient city of Nikaia (Nicaea), was founded in 316 B.C. by Antigonos, one of Alexander the Great's generals, later becoming capital of the Kingdom of Bithynia. Occupied in time by the Romans the city prospered, but in A.D. 259 it was sacked and burned by the Goths. Under the Emperor Constantine Nicaea achieved special prominence as the meeting-place of the first Ecumenical Council (A.D. 325). From 1080 to 1097 it was capital of the Seljuk Empire, and following a period in the hands of the Crusaders was then metropolis of the Byzantine Empire from 1204 until 1261. It was captured by the Ottomans in 1331.

From 1331 until the 17th c. Iznik was the Ottoman centre for tile making. The

Iznik (Nicaea)

Green Mosque in Bursa, a number of other mosques, and several rooms in the Topkapi Seraya in Istanbul are amongst the many buildings decorated with tiles made in Iznik.

 From the Roman and Byzantine Periods

Bearing witness to the historical importance of Iznik are a number of buildings from different periods:

The 4.5 km-long town walls, only parts of which are well preserved, date back to Roman times. There are inner and outer walls and numerous towers and gates. Of the four main gates, the Lefka (east) Gate and the Istanbul Gate have best withstood the many sieges and burnings. There are also remains of a Roman theatre from the time of Hadrian.

Surviving from the Byzantine period are the ruins of the Iznik Hagia Sophia (meeting-place in 787 of the seventh Ecumenical Council), the 8th to 11th c. Koimesis Church, decorated with floor mosaics and 11th c. frescoes, and the 6th c. aqueduct, part of which is still in use.

The finest example of Ottoman architecture in Iznik is the Green Mosque, built in 1387. The minaret is still completely faced with tiles, and the portal is richly ornamented.

Much the earliest manifestations of past cultures are the two graves with ornamental, coloured wall decorations, discovered in 1967 on the Elbeyli road a little way from Iznik and about 2300 years old. Viewing can be arranged through the Iznik Museum.

The museum, housed in the Nilüfer Hatun Imareti (the former charity kitchen), has on display Greek, Roman and Byzantine antiquities as well as Iznik tiles. It is definitely worth seeing.

 From Istanbul-Kabatas to Yalova; then by bus or dolmus to Iznik (60 km).

 Fish restaurant at Lake Iznik.

  at Lake Iznik.

 Simple camping sites by the lake.

The Dardanelles

Like the Bosporus the Dardanelles have always been an important waterway, not only strategically and economically as a shipping route between the Mediterranean and the Black Sea but also as a boundary between the continents of Europe and Asia. The Persian army of King Xerxes crossed the strait, then known as the Hellespont, in 480 B.C., as did Alexander the Great with his army in 334 B.C.. The Emperor Barbarossa and his Crusaders crossed in 1190, followed later by the Ottoman's when making their first incursion into Europe. At various times control of the Dardanelles has been fought over by the Venetians, Turks, Russians and British. In the First World War, fighting on the side of the German and Austro-Hungarian empires, the Turks successfully defended the strait against the allied forces. After 1936 the Treaties of Lausanne and Montreux secured free passage for merchant shipping of all nations and for warships belonging to the Black Sea states.

Signs of a troubled past are still evident on both sides of the Dardanelles; these range from Classical ruins to First World War trenches. At the head of the Gallipoli Peninsula on the European side (to the left when approaching from the Mediterranean) is the small town of Dardanos, an ancient Greek settlement from which the Dardanelles later took their name. There is also a huge monument to Atatürk. On a clear day the hills of Troy can be seen rising above the plain on the Asiatic side.

Scenically the Dardanelles are most striking at their narrowest point, near Çanakkale, where two 15th c. fortresses stand facing one another. The fortifications on the Asiatic shore were built by Sultan Mehmet II while the European shore opposite is guarded by the smaller Kilidülbahir Fort. In Çanakkale (pop. 30,000), a provincial capital on the Asiatic side, there is a small archaeological museum, and the Turkish soldiers who lost their lives in the battle for the Dardanelles during the First World War are commemorated by a 40 m-high monument. A car ferry operates between Çanakkale and Eceabat, connecting the two continents. Çanakkale is also the departure-point for coach excursions to Troy, only 40 km away.

Where the Dardanelles enter the Sea of Marmara the little fishing port of Gelibolu (pop. 16,000) lies on the European side. This was once a Greek colony called Callipolis, later Gallipoli. From the water the ruins of a Byzantine fortress can be seen.

Troy

Written in the 8th c. B.C. Homer's epic poem 'The Iliad', recounting the stories of the Greek heroes, has made Troy one of the most famous settings in

Troy

world literature. For ten long years the Greeks besieged the city because Paris, a Trojan prince, had abducted the beautiful Helen, wife of the King of Sparta. Despite their bravery and persistence, the Greeks — or Danaans as Homer called them — were unable to take the city until they acted on the cunning advice of Odysseus. Feigning retreat they left outside the city walls a large wooden horse, the legendary 'Trojan Horse', apparently as a peace offering. Within the hollow body of the horse Greek warriors were concealed. In jubilation the Trojans pulled the offering into the city, and with it the enemy. Troy was destroyed.

The stories of these people continue to fascinate, and the names of Achilles, Agamemnon, Odysseus and Priam remain familiar to everyone; but the scene and action of Homer's epic were long thought to be based merely on legend. In total defiance of accepted opinion, however, the 19th c. German businessman turned archaeologist Heinrich Schliemann was convinced that Homer must have been writing about historical events, and in 1870 he discovered and excavated the remains of the city.

As a result of excavation nine layers have now been differentiated (levels I - IX), of which levels II and VI are the most important; level IX represents the last phase of rebuilding in Roman times. Archaeologists have been able to show that Troy was indeed attacked and destroyed by the Achaian Greeks around 1200 B.C. (level VIIa). It is very probable that Homer based his tale on this attack. Apart from the nine levels there is little to interest the non-expert on the site of the excavations. Archaeological finds from the area, however, are on display in a small museum.

Troy

Black Sea Coast

The Black Sea coast of Turkey is not nearly as well known as the holiday resorts of Bulgaria and Rumania, but the Turkish landscape is even more delightful, being green and mountainous, and the climate is also more favourable, hence the cultivation of both tea and tobacco. The disadvantages are the greater distance and the extreme shortage of holiday accommodation up to international standards.

Black Sea resorts which can be recommended are Kilyos, Şile, Akçakoca and Amasra. Zonguldak is a major port but there is nothing much to see there. Sinop on the other hand is well worth visiting, as too is Samsun by anyone interested in modern Turkish history. Since stretches of the coastal road are still under construction much the best way to get to these towns is by sea, with the Turkish shipping company Denizyollari.

Beyond Samsun, between Ünye, Ordu and Giresun in eastern Anatolia (not covered by this guide), is the 'Hazelnut Coast', so called because of its hazelnut groves. It was from Giresun that the Roman general and gourmet Lucullus introduced the first cherry tree into Europe. The historic port of Trabzon (formerly Trebizond) and the town of Rize at the eastern end of the Black Sea are centres of an intensive tea-growing area.

Kilyos Pop. 5000

Kilyos is the only seaside resort on the European side of the Turkish Black Sea coast. Because of its proximity to Istanbul it is overcrowded and comparatively expensive.

 Fine sandy beach: admission about 60p, beach hut about £1.80. There are also sandy beaches surrounded by high dunes at Demirciköy and Gemüsdere. Beware of dangerous eddies when bathing.

 In the Motel *Kilyos* and in many small restaurants.

 Good bus connections to Istanbul and for excursions on the Bosporus.

Şile Pop. 9000

On the Asiatic side the nearest resort to Istanbul is Şile, 75 km away. It too is a favourite with the people of Istanbul, though it is less crowded than Kilyos.

 Beautiful sandy beach at Kumbaba, 3 km away.

 Especially in Kumbaba; no radios are allowed on the beach.

  Hotel *Degirmen*.

 Lovely hand-embroidered blouses.

 Bus connection to Istanbul in summer.

Akçakoca Pop. 12,000

Akçakoca, a small town set in wooded, hilly surroundings, is the first port of call after Istanbul for Black Sea steamers. Hazelnuts are also grown there.

 Several small sand and pebble beaches separated by green hillsides. Changing huts and awnings. Beautiful beach at the promontory near Karaburun (6 km).

 Several.

Amasra Pop. 5000

Situated on a headland, the very picturesque small port of Amasra is overlooked by a Byzantine citadel, the ramparts of which are still well preserved. Archaeological finds from the surrounding area are on display in the small but interesting museum. There is still no holiday accommodation to speak of in Amasra but the beaches are much used by people from Ankara.

Traditional Turkish embroidery

 Sandy beach in the large harbour, pebble beach in the small harbour; the nicest beach is 3 km away at Inkum.

 Wood carvings.

 By river-boat to Bartin (11 km), through a gorge on the river Filyos; by Black Sea steamer to Sinop.

Sinop Pop. 20,000

Built on a narrow peninsula, the small fishing port of Sinop possesses one of the finest natural harbours on the Turkish Black Sea coast, which accounts for its continuing importance since antiquity.

Birthplace of the philosopher Diogenes

The Greek philosopher Diogenes was born at Sinop in 413 B.C.. From here also, or perhaps from Trabzon, the survivors of an army of over ten thousand embarked for Greece in 399 B.C. following a disastrous expedition to Mesopotamia. Their leader Cyrus having died, the soldier-historian Xenophon led a heroic retreat during which the army suffered great deprivation. In 1854 the destruction of the Turkish fleet at Sinop brought the outbreak of the Crimean War.

On exhibition in the town park museum are Greek, Roman, Byzantine and Ottoman artefacts, icons, carpets from the 16th to 18th centuries, and a collection of folk art. Next to the museum the remains of a 2nd c. B.C. temple have been excavated. A considerable part of the town wall remains standing, dating from the Byzantine and Genoese periods. The Büyük Cami, its mausoleum and the Koranic school with its richly decorated portal all date from the 13th c. There is also a row of delightful old wooden houses.

Several beaches near the town.

Samsun Pop. 200,000

Samsun, the Amisos of antiquity and now the largest city on the Turkish Black Sea coast, is a major port and industrial town, and a tobacco-growing centre. The liberation of Turkey from foreign occupation began at Samsun in 1919 when Atatürk landed there, an event commemorated by the Atatürk Monument in the town park and by an Atatürk Museum. A festival is held annually on the anniversary of Atatürk's arrival (May 19th). There is a fine panoramic view from Acropolis Hill, almost 300 m high.

 Very good sandy beaches about 12 km west of the town.

    Hotel *Grand Samsun*.

The Castle of St Peter, Bodrum

The Aegean Coast and Hinterland

The Turkish Aegean coast extends from Çanakkale, on the Asiatic side of the Dardanelles at their narrowest point, south as far as Fethiye. The Turks take great pride in quoting Herodotus who described its sky as the most beautiful and its climate as the best in the world.

The Aegean coast is still the most well known and most visited holiday area in Turkey, its numerous ancient sites, Ephesus and Pergamon in particular, being part of its attraction.

The Greeks and Romans found conditions in western and southern Anatolia entirely familiar. A number of Greek tribes established colonial cities here which often grew to surpass those of their native homeland in size and beauty. The Romans took over most of these cities, altering and extending them to suit their needs. Roman generals and rulers seem to have been attracted to the provinces of Asia Minor and many well-known men worked and built there — but also wrought considerable destruction.

The coastal regions of Turkey were also the primary destination and sphere of activity for the early Christian apostles and saints. But the peoples already established in Asiatic Turkey and those who poured in from eastern Turkey have also left their mark.

Turkish soil conceals a wealth of material from times gone by, but since the interest in archaeology blossomed in the 19th c. only a small part of the riches have been uncovered. The fate of the Pergamon altar is typical of what befell the art treasures discovered in those early days, many of them being removed from the excavation sites to be scattered and exhibited in museums all over Europe. While the Turks have always resented seeing these treasures dispersed abroad it was only in this way that interest was created and money raised for further excavations. Today, the Turkish government strictly protects its archaeological treasures and takes responsibility for the continuing research which is carried on with international support.

For some years now the Aegean coast has faced increasing competition from the south coast of Turkey, which is being systematically developed and which is also well-endowed with ancient sites of major importance. In an attempt to keep ahead the Aegean coastal resorts have striven hard to become ever more accessible to tourism and there are direct flights from the UK to Izmir and Dalaman.

Interesting excursions can be made from all the Aegean coastal resorts to sites usually within a short distance. There are also ferry services and excursions to most of the Greek islands lying off the coast, although when, as at present, relations between Turkey and Greece are strained, the opportunities for such excursions become limited. Drivers must expect poor roads in this part of the country, and the rocky terrain makes seemingly never ending detours necessary.

Here it is only possible to give some basic details of the main sightseeing attractions and the seaside resorts most likely to interest British tourists.

Edremit Pop. 26,000

Edremit and its seaside suburbs Akçay and Ören lie in a bay on the north-west corner of the Aegean coast almost surrounded by olive groves. Up until now it has served mainly as a holiday destination for the Turks, but it also has an international youth holiday centre and some category 1 and 2 motels.

The best beach is at Akçay.

H Thermal springs and the remains of a Roman bath.

♫ In the *Akçay Tatil Köyü* holiday village and in the *Efem* Motel in Ören.

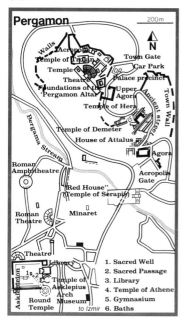

1. Sacred Well
2. Sacred Passage
3. Library
4. Temple of Athene
5. Gymnasium
6. Baths

⛺ At Ören.

🚌 To the Acropolis of Assos (75 km west near Ayvacik) where there are the remains of a 6th c. B.C. Temple of Athena.

To the Şeytan Sofrasi (Devil's Dining Table), 55 km south-west on the Sarimsakli peninsula near Ayvalik, from where there is a panoramic view of the bay and the group of small islands called the Maden Islands.

Dikili/Pergamon

The sleepy little harbour town of Dikili is not itself particularly interesting, but it is the starting point for excursions to Pergamon, 30 km inland.

Built among the ruins of the ancient city of Pergamon, which in Classical times had up to 160,000 inhabitants, is the small provincial town of Bergama, population 30,000. Approaching by road there is a spectacular view of the ancient acropolis or upper city, stretching out on Castle Hill almost 300 m above the modern town. It is a sight difficult to match.

🏛 Capital of the Pergamon Empire

Until the 3rd c. B.C. Pergamon was merely a small settlement. During the Hellenistic period it expanded under Attalid rule into the rich and magnificent capital of the Pergamon 'empire', later bequeathed to the Romans in 133 B.C. by Attalus III. Most of the remains on Castle Hill date from Pergamon's 'Period of Greatness', but even after the empire had become a Roman province the city continued to be culturally influential. It was one of the most important early Christian

Asklepieion

communities and is mentioned, together with other Christian centres including Ephesus, in the Book of Revelation of St John.

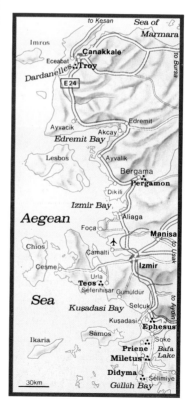

Acropolis and Asklepieion

Acropolis. The most impressive sights are the remains of the ancient terraces and their retaining walls, and the acropolis with its palaces, gateways and temples. In the acropolis the Altar of Zeus and the library are particularly famous. Only the foundations of the altar can still now be seen (there is a reconstruction based on the original frieze in the Pergamon Museum in East Berlin). The library was founded by King Attalus I. Its 200,000 parchment volumes — the use of parchment is believed to have originated in Pergamon — were later presented by Mark Anthony to Cleopatra after the library at Alexandria burnt down. The Roman theatre, with its eighty rows of seating most of which has survived (capable of accommodating some 14,000 spectators), was built into the very steep slope of Castle Hill.

Asklepieion. Across the town from the acropolis, on the other side of the stream which runs through Bergama, a well preserved colonnaded avenue leads to the ruins of the Asklepieion. Here there is another library, a sacred well, an underground passage, two round temples, and a theatre in which an arts festival is now held annually in mid-May. After Kos and Epidauros the Pergamon Asklepieion was the most celebrated place of healing in the Hellenistic world. The round Temple of Telephoros was the treatment centre, offering a combination of nature cure — medicinal herbs, mud baths and sunbathing were among the remedies used — and hypnotic suggestion, the state of trance probably being induced by opium vapours.

Bergama

In the modern town the Archaeological Museum and the Red Basilica are especially worth visiting. The museum has a fine collection of Greek and Roman sculptures, and bronze and clay figures. The ruined basilica, also known as the Red Courtyard, is a very unusual red-brick structure, built by the Emperor Hadrian as a temple to the Egyptian god Serapis but converted later into a Christian basilica.

Foça Pop. 3000

Foça (also known as Eski Foça), the ancient Phocaea, is a jewel of the north Aegean coast. The peaceful, well kept little port has so far escaped being over-run by tourism. In the picturesque nar-row streets the typical sandstone houses with red-tiled roofs are now protected buildings. The scenery on the headlands and along the coast is very varied, with oddly shaped rocks, groves of fruit trees, meadows and fields. Most fascinating of all is the Sirens' Isle with its fantastic rock formations. There is a Club Méditerranée village 6 km from Foça.

    Sandy beaches and rocky shores either side of Foça.

  Several small restaurants along the harbour front.

  Festival in late July with music, folk dancing and water sports.

Izmir

  To Izmir, 60 km, and Pergamon, 50 km.

Izmir Pop. 800,000

Situated mid-way down the Aegean coast, Izmir is Turkey's third largest city and second largest port after Istanbul, a place of call for numerous cruise liners whose passengers spill ashore to make excursions to Ephesus and Pergamon. Izmir is also a popular and reasonably priced shopping centre, essential sightseeing itself, and an excellent base for exploring Turkey's past. It is wholly unsuitable for bathing, however; sewage from the city (which together with its environs has some 1.5 million inhabitants) flows into the large bay. The nearest safe bathing beach is at Inciralti, 12 km to the west.

That said, Izmir should certainly not be missed. Atop the ancient Mount Pagos the Kadifekale Fortress provides the best view of the city and the bay round which it is built.

The rulers of Smyrna

In the suburb of Bayrakli, excavation of Tepekule Hill has exposed the remains of a 5000-year-old settlement which de-veloped during antiquity into the

Greek colonial capital of Smyrna. Destroyed by the Lydians and captured first by the Medes and then the Persians, the city flourished with the coming of Alexander the Great. Later the Romans ruled the thriving metropolis, giving way in turn to the Byzantines, followed by the Seljuks, Crusaders and Genoese. In the 15th c. the city was incorporated into the Ottoman Empire. It was at Smyrna that the Greek invasion took place at the start of the war between Turkey and Greece (1919–1922), and it was Atatürk's recovery of the city on September 9th 1922 which brought the Turkish War of Independence to a successful conclusion.

 Little now survives as a legacy of Smyrna's ancient past; only the restored agora (marketplace), which has fine statues of Demeter and Poseidon and some free-standing columns; the remains of the Kadifekale Fortress, originally built by Alexander the Great's general Lysimachos but rebuilt by Marcus Aurelius after an earthquake in A.D. 178; and the Greek, Roman and Byzantine exhibits in the Archaeological Museum.

✈ Daily flights connect Izmir with Ankara and Istanbul and there is a weekly flight to Antalya. There are also flights from the UK. Several shipping lines call regularly at Izmir.

⤳ At the luxury *Efes* Hotel.

⊗ In the *Efes, Etap* and other hotels.

✗ Plenty of good eating places, especially in the Old Town and along the Kordon, the wide sea-front promenade.

🍸 🎵 The most elegant surroundings are in the *Efes* Hotel; several more venues in the Culture Park and on the Cumhuriyet Bulvari.

🎷 In the *Efes* Hotel.

✂ The International Mediterranean Festival in June, with folk music and dancing from a number of different countries. Izmir International Fair in August/September.

🧺 Particularly leather clothes, articles of gold and silver, alabaster ware, carpets and Smyrna figs; all to be found in the bazaar, along the nearby Anafartalar Street, and on the sea-front.

⛺ *BP Mocamp Inciralti,* 12 km from the city centre on the Cesme road; also at the *Afacan* Motel on the E 24.

🚌 To Manisa, 45 km to the northeast, with its Murat Mosque built by Sinan, its museum, the Great Mosque (Ulu Cami) into which ancient columns were incorporated, and the Sultan's Mosque. Some 7 km east of Manisa is a badly weathered relief, believed to have been carved into the rock in about the 15th c. B.C. and possibly representing the Hittite goddess Cybele.

To the ruins of the former Lydian capital of Sardis — at Sart, 105 km to the east — with the remains of a celebrated Temple of Artemis, a restored Roman gymnasium, and an avenue of Roman columns.

To Ephesus (75 km) and Pergamon (110 km), taking one of the organised tours.

Urla Pop. 12,000

Urla is a small town to the west of Izmir. Urla itself is a kilometre or two inland, but there is a landing-place at Urla Iskelesi. There are new holiday villages nearby.

� 🎵 In the *Nebioglu* holiday village near Urla, in a sandy bay surrounded by cliffs.

✗ In Urla.

🚌 To Izmir (30 km). Set out from Seferihisar (35 km) for the little port of Sigacik with its Genoese fortress and modern marina and to the lonely ruins of the ancient city of Teos, where there was once a Temple of Dionysos.

Çeşme Pop. 8000

The Çeşme Peninsula west of Izmir offers a wide selection of tourist hotels, bungalows and apartments, especially around Çeşme and Ilica. There is a marina at Altin Yünüz where the holiday village also caters for water sports. The fishing village of Çeşme is a holiday and health resort, with thermal baths. The centre of the village is dominated by a great 15th c. Genoese fortress.

 Sandy and rocky beaches on either side of Çeşme; the sand is wonderfully fine on the beaches at Ilica (5 km), at the *Golden Dolphin* holiday village (5 km), and at the *Çeşme Grand Oteli* (7 km, with showers and changing huts on the beach).

H Thermal sulphur springs, reputed to be effective in the treatment of rheumatism, sciatica and neuralgia.

 Large heated swimming pool at the *Çeşme Grand Oteli*.

 Golden Dolphin

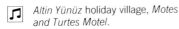 *Altin Yünüz* holiday village, *Motes and Turtes Motel*.

 To Seferihisar (60 km) and Izmir (85 km). Boat trips to the Greek island of Chios.

Gümüldür (or Gümüşsuyu) Pop. 1000

On a poor road off the E 24 between Izmir and Ephesus the village of Gümüldür would be of little interest were it not for the nearby hotel and bungalow complexes, the *Sultan* and the *Paşa*. Situated in isolated, sandy bays surrounded by cliffs, both developments, but especially the *Sultan*, offer many holiday facilities including table tennis, mini-golf and children's playgrounds.

 Sultan and Paşa

 30 minutes to Kesre, a delightful Anatolian mountain village.

 Boat trip to Klaros to see the ruins of the now partly submerged Temple of Apollo and the oracle chamber beneath it. By car or bus to Izmir (50 km).

Kuşadasi Pop. 15,000

After Alanya, Kuşadasi is the best known and most popular international resort on the Turkish coast. It is beautifully situated in a large bay, with innumerable separate coves. The heavily wooded hills of the hinterland and the Greek island of Samos opposite add to the attractiveness of its setting, scenery in which the intensity of the light and the glowing sunsets become all the more spectacular.

Despite its 2000 years of history Kuşadasi itself has no ancient ruins; but it is not far from the ancient sites of Ephesus, Priene, Miletus and Didyma. The resort's most interesting buildings are the heavily fortified 16th c. Ottoman caravanserai (now a hotel) and the reasonably well-preserved Ottoman fortress on Pigeon Island, connected to the mainland by a causeway.

Kuşadasi is a popular port of call for cruise ships with passengers visiting Ephesus. Fortunately, despite the busy tourist trade, the town has managed to retain its oriental character and charm, with little coffee-houses, a small bazaar, Turkish baths and the muezzin calling the people to prayer.

 On both sides of the town sandy beaches alternate with rocky shores and concrete terraces, with steps down into the sea.

 In the *Kismet, Imbat* and *Tusan* hotels.

Souvenirs on sale in Kuşadasi

 Marina with yacht charter and hire.

 In the hotels.

 Several restaurants.

 In the *Kismet* and *Imbat* hotels, and at the *Ömer* holiday village. Bar on Pigeon Island.

 At least once a week during the holiday season.

Two large holiday centres have been built near Kuşadasi. The *Club Mediterranée* (4 km to the south) is open only to members.

Plenty to do at the *Kuştur* holiday village 5 km north of Kuşadasi:

 Horses and camels.

 To Ephesus and Selçuk 20 km, Priene 40 km, Miletus 62 km, Didyma 75 km and Izmir 90 km; by car or on organised tours. During the holiday season there are daily ferries to the Greek island of Samos — just so long as political relations are cordial on both sides.

Ephesus and Selçuk

Owing to silting by the Little Maeander river (Kücük Menderes, the River Kaystros of antiquity), the former port of Ephesus now lies 6 km inland. It is from the loops in the river's course that the word 'meander' clearly derives.

 A rich trading city

The name of Ephesus is familiar to many people from the Apostle Paul's Epistle to the Ephesians. Indeed Ephesus played an important part in the history of Christianity. Paul lived here for three years, the Apostle John worked in the community, and Mary is even said to have come to Ephesus after Jesus' death. It was also the meeting-place for the ecumenical council held in A.D. 431.

In the pre-Christian era the Greek colonial city on the site was of great economic, cultural and political importance. The earliest traces date back some 3500 years. In Roman times the rich trading port with its prosperous harbour was capital of the Roman province of Asia, with a

Ephesus

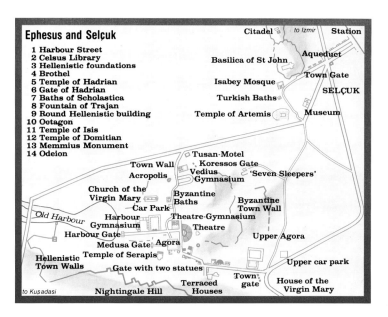

Ephesus and Selçuk

1 Harbour Street
2 Celsus Library
3 Hellenistic foundations
4 Brothel
5 Temple of Hadrian
6 Gate of Hadrian
7 Baths of Scholastica
8 Fountain of Trajan
9 Round Hellenistic building
10 Octagon
11 Temple of Isis
12 Temple of Domitian
13 Memmius Monument
14 Odeion

Citadel   to Izmir   Station

Basilica of St John   Aqueduct

Town Gate

Isabey Mosque

SELÇUK

Turkish Baths

Temple of Artemis   Museum

Tusan-Motel

Town Wall   Koressos Gate

Acropolis   Vedius   'Seven Sleepers'
    Gymnasium

Church of the   Byzantine
Virgin Mary   Baths   Byzantine
    Town Wall
Car Park
Old Harbour   Theatre-Gymnasium
    Harbour   Theatre
    Gymnasium
    Harbour Gate   Upper Agora

Medusa Gate   Agora

Hellenistic   Temple of Serapis
Town Walls   Gate with two statues   Upper car park

to Kuşadası   Nightingale Hill   Terraced   Town   House of the
    Houses   gate   Virgin Mary

population sometimes in excess of 200,000. Until the coming of Christianity the famous Temple of Artemis at Ephesus was the most important centre of the cult of Artemis in the eastern Mediterranean. The city's flourishing intellectual life produced a number of great thinkers including the philosopher Heraclitus (540–480 B.C.) who lived here.

Archaeological finds

Tours of the site usually start from the entrance in the lower car park (restaurant etc.) close by the remains of the Theatre Gymnasium. Immediately beyond the Gymnasium a wide thoroughfare (Harbour Street or the 'Arcadian Way', built in the 4th c. A.D. and once graced by triumphal gateways at each end) leads west past the Harbour Gymnasium (on the right) to where the Old Harbour once was. A short distance north of the Harbour

Gymnasium (close once again to the lower car park) lie the ruins of the Double Church, or Church of the Virgin Mary. It was here that the Third Ecumenical Council met in 431, raising the doctrine of Mary as Mother of God to the status of a dogma. At its eastern end Harbour Street leads to the Great Theatre with seating for an audience of 25,000, in which the Apostle Paul is said to have preached. From the Theatre, Marble Street runs southwards, past the Lower Agora (market) and two very fine Celsus Library on the right and into the Street of the Curetes which bears left to the east car park and entrance. Starting from the lower end, the main buildings on either side of the Street of the Curetes are: on the left the ancient brothel, the Temple of Hadrian, the Baths of Scholastica and the Fountain of Trajan, and on the right the Octagon tomb and some terraced houses with frescos. The street leads up to a plateau on the hilltop where there are remains of the Upper Agora with its little Temple of Isis, the Temple of Domitian immediately west of it, and on its north side the Monument to Caius Memmius and the Odeion.

Winding round the slopes of Bülbül Daği (Nightingale Hill) on the southern edge of the site are remains of the old Hellenistic city walls. In a wood on nearby Ala Daği is a small building revealed in a vison to the German nun Katherina Emmerich as the house in which the Virgin Mary lived and died. The house is now a place of veneration for both Christians and Moslems and a service is held every year on August 15th celebrating the Assumption.

The most famous building in old Ephesus, one of the Seven Wonders of the ancient world, the Temple of Artemis, the goddess of fertility, stood between Ephesus and the existing small town of Selçuk. Nothing remains of the temple (6th c. B.C.) except a depression in the ground.

At Selçuk the museum houses the main archaeological finds from Ephesus which include statues of Artemis, and the celebrated bronze 'Boy with the Dolphin'. Citadel Hill, with its massive Seljuk fortress and the ruined Basilica of St John, occupies a commanding position over the little town.

Also noteworthy at Selçuk are the 'Gate of Persecution', a Byzantine city gate decorated with a fine relief, and the large 14th c. Isa Bey Mosque with high walls, a spacious inner courtyard and richly ornamented portal.

Cultural and arts festival in Selçuk and Ephesus in early May (with theatre and folk dancing, some in the Great Theatre at Ephesus). Camel fights are held in the country district between Selçuk and Aydin (80 km to the east) from January to April.

Information bureau in Selçuk at the small bazaar opposite the museum.

Priene, Miletus and Didyma

Beyond Söke on the main highway south from Kuşadasi a road turns off south-westwards to the ruins of the ancient Carian cities of Priene (40 km from Kuşadasi), Miletus (62 km) and Didyma (75 km).

Priene reached the peak of its prosperity under the Lydians and at the time of Alexander the Great. It is built on a series of terraces above the valley of the Menderes (Meander), overlooked by a sheer marble crag, an outlier of the Samsun Daği massif (the Mt Mykale of antiquity). The town was laid out mainly in the 4th c. B.C., the architect Hippodamos adopting a square grid system which is now most clearly visible from the vantage point of the Theatre, itself of great interest with its marble altar and bench of honour. The Temple of Athena almost demands to be photographed, a row of 5 Ionic columns (rebuilt) rising skyward against a backdrop of steep crags. The ruins of ancient dwelling houses, the Agora, the Gymnasium and the Bouleuterion or Council Chamber should also be seen. The climb to the acropolis on top of the marble crag (371 m) above the town is very hard work and there are virtually no ancient remains to reward the effort.

Miletus (Miletos) was, from the 8th c. B.C. to the 6th c. A.D., the largest Greek city in Asia Minor. The site is strewn with remains of foundations and walls (of baths, an agora, a stadium, a Temple of Athena, a Byzantine castle and so on), but only the well-preserved Theatre with seating for 30,000 people creates any real impression.

From the 9th or 10th c. B.C. Miletus, at that time a coastal city — now 10 km inland, surrounded by the flood plain of the Little Maeander (Küçük Menderes) — was an important port and commercial and cultural centre. During a series of disputes with the Lydians, Persians, Macedonians and Romans it

Priene

was destroyed and rebuilt many times, remaining powerful until the 3rd c. A.D. During the Crusades it began to thrive once again, but fell into final decline under the Ottomans and was ultimately abandoned.

Didyma. At one time even more renowned than the Delphic oracle, the oracle at Didyma dates back to the 10th c. B.C., and from the 3rd c. B.C. was linked to Miletus, 20 km away, by a 'Sacred Way'. The extensive and impressive ruins of the great Temple of Apollo also date from the 3rd c. B.C., the magnitude of the temple being easily appreciated from the columns and remains of walls still standing, the stumps of the almost complete double colonnade and the elaborately decorated cornices now lying on the ground. At the entrance to the temple site are a fine Medusa's head and Hellenistic lion.

At Altinkum, 5 km south of Didyma, there is a pleasant, sandy beach.

Herakleia on Lake Bafa

The ruins of Herakleia, a city built by the Carians and Greeks, lie in an area of wild and desolate scenery, this actually being the main attraction of a visit to the site. Although quite a lot has survived — a considerable part of the old city walls with their ruined towers and narrow arches, the remains of a small

Didyma

The Castle of St Peter, Bodrum

Temple of Athena, a theatre and a number of Carian tombs — nothing here can really be said to be essential sightseeing. The tombs hewn in the rock on either side of the approach road are also very difficult to find.

Amidst the rubble of Herakleia, on the rugged slopes of Mt Latmos above Lake Bafa, there is a truly picturesque little mountain village whose inhabitants still wear traditional costume as part of their everyday life.

To reach Herakleia take the road from Kuşadasi through Söke, continuing towards Milas until past Lake Bafa. Turn left at a signpost on the outskirts of the tiny village of Bafa (just a few houses), down an unmetalled road to the lake.

Bodrum Pop. 7000

Bodrum, the ancient Halicarnassos (home of Herodotus the 'father' of European history), lies on the north side of the Gulf of Gökova at the neck of a small peninsula which extends westwards towards the Greek islands of Kalimnos and Kos. It is an exceptionally pleasant small town with an oval-shaped harbour speckled with the sails of yachts, around which pretty whitewashed cottages climb the green terraced hillside in a patchwork of palms, vineyards and colourful gardens. Bodrum Bay is dominated by a large, somewhat lumpish 15th c. Crusader fortress, the Castle of St Peter, built on the former islet of Zephyron now joined to the shore. Souvenir shops, boutiques, coffee and tea-houses and taverns give Bodrum a real holiday atmosphere. From June to September it is especially popular with the Turks themselves, though the marina with berths for 140 yachts and the growing number of cruise ships which moor in the harbour give it more of a cosmopolitan air.

In the Castle of St Peter (Bodrum Kalesi), especially in the Knights' Hall and the former chapel, is an important museum which includes finds from vessels sunk off Bodrum. One of its finest exhibits is a bronze statue of the goddess Isis from the 2nd c. B.C.

In antiquity Bodrum could boast one of the Seven Wonders of the ancient world, the 4th c. B.C. tomb of the Persian ruler of Halicarnassos, Mausolos (from whose name and burial place the word mausoleum derives). Important remains from the tomb are now in the British Museum, among them statues of Mausolos and his wife Artemisia, and one of the horses from the quadriga (a chariot drawn by four horses abreast) which crowned the building. Only restored remnants of the foundations are to be seen in Bodrum.

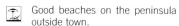 Good beaches on the peninsula outside town.

In the new holiday village at Torba Bay.

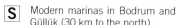 **S** Modern marinas in Bodrum and Güllük (30 km to the north).

In the Hotel *Halicarnassos* and the T.M.T. holiday village.

Bodrum is a good place to buy local products, ranging from blue pearls (typical of Bodrum) and real sponges to leather goods and textiles, and hand-knotted carpets from Milas, a town inland. There is a market in Bodrum on Fridays.

▲ *Ayaz-Camping*, 3 km to the west.

Cultural and arts festival in the first week in September.

Half-day and day excursions to the Bodrum Peninsula with its luxuriant vegetation, secluded bays and beaches, little fishing villages, and small farming communities surrounded by orchards and olive groves.

To Milas, formerly Mylasa the capital of ancient Caria, 67 km from Bodrum on

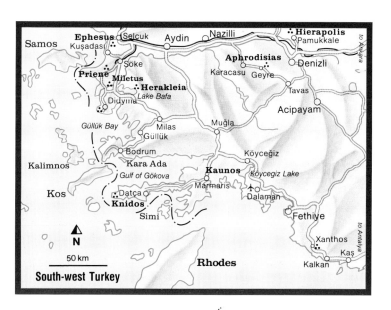

South-west Turkey

Marmaris on the Aegean Coast

the road to Söke; there is a pre-Christian arch decorated with the Carian double axe, a Roman mausoleum with twelve columns, other ancient ruins and a mosque dating back to the 14th c.

A further 13 km beyond Milas to the ruined Temple of Euromos which has 16 Corinthian columns; another 50 km to Miletus, or 60 km to Didyma.

Boat trips to the island of Kara Ada ('Black Island') 8 km from Bodrum, where there is a grotto with a thermal spring in which to bathe. *Mavi Yolculuk* (Blue Voyage) cruises through the beautiful scenery of the Gulf of Gökova. By boat to the Greek island of Kos.

Kaunos rock tombs, Dalyan, Köyceğiz

Marmaris Pop. 6000

Marmaris lies surrounded by wooded hills on the landward end of a narrow peninsula forming the southern shore of the Gulf of Gökova. In antiquity Phykos, as the town was then called, was a prosperous trading port but scarcely any traces of this period have been found. The ruins of a small fortress and a caravanserai date from the 16th c.

Today Marmaris is one of the busiest and most popular holiday resorts on the Turkish Aegean coast, with good hotels and motels and a beautiful holiday village in a pine forest by the sea. It has good shops, coffee-houses and restaurants.

 Pebble and sandy beaches along the wooded shore, including some shallow ones suitable for children. (A small admission fee is sometimes charged.)

 Children's playground in the *Marmaris holiday village* (also table tennis, volleyball, minigolf etc.).

  Marina.

 Hotel *Marti*.

 Hotel *Marti* and the *Marmaris holiday village*.

Hotel *Marti* (also Turkish specialities).

Hotel *Marti,* the *Marmaris holiday village*, Hotel *Lidya* and several discothèques on the sea-front.

To the provincial capital Muğla 60 km to the north (especially for the Thursday market).

To Köyceğiz 65 km north-east, a village at the head of Lake Köyceğiz (20 km long) which runs into the sea through a very narrow channel; another 25 km to Dalyan on the lake's outlet to the sea, where there are some good simple seafood restaurants. Boat from Dalyan through narrow waterways, the banks lined with tall reeds and canes, to the ancient site of Kaunos where there are impressive rock tombs, the foundations of a theatre, and Roman baths.

Boat trips to Cleopatra Island and elsewhere in the Bay of Marmaris.

By boat to the Greek island of Rhodes (about 3 hours).

Datça Pop. 1000

Datça is a small fishing village and artists' community 80 km west of Marmaris, perched on a narrow neck of land some 90 km long. Accommodation is limited but there are nice restaurants, souvenir shops, a marina and a sandy beach.

Datça is also the departure-point for excursions by boat or car to the ancient Greek city of Knidos (35 km) at the end of the peninsula, the site of some well-preserved Hellenistic walls, the remains of two theatres and a round temple. Excavation there is still in progress.

Fethiye Pop. 9000

Fethiye, an important port since the time of the Lycian Empire (13th to 4th

By the rock tombs of Fethiye

Left: Fethiye. Above: Pamukkale

c. B.C.) when it was called Telmessos, now exports significant quantities of chromium ore. It has also developed into a thriving holiday resort, especially popular for its large beautiful beaches (unfortunately very crowded) and its setting in a bay enclosed by mountains and dotted with small islands. Drawing visitors with an interest in history to Fethiye are the temple-like Lycian rock tombs — 6th to 4th c. B.C. — hewn high up in the steep rock face east of the town.

  There is a good road from Muğla and Antalya; and steamer connections to Antalya and Izmir.

 Excursions by boat to the little islands and deserted beaches in Fethiye Bay; to the neighbouring Belceğiz Bay (a small town with delightful beaches, restaurants, camping sites and thermal baths), and to an island offshore with Byzantine ruins. By car (17 km) or boat to the turquoise waters and pine forests of the Ülü Deniz lagoon (for excellent bathing and lots of water-sports). To the particularly beautiful coastal nature reserve south-west of Fethiye, with its backdrop of the Bey Mountains.

To Xanthos, 60 km along the Kaş road (see Kaş).

Pamukkale and Hierapolis Alt. 340 m; Pop. 2000

Of the longer excursions, a trip to Pamukkale must be the top priority for any visitor to the Aegean coast. It is reached most easily from Kuşadasi taking the E 24 via Aydin and Denizli (about 210 km). From Fethiye, Marmaris, Bodrum, and other southern Aegean resorts that route is also the best, driving north on the main Muğla road to join the E 24 at Aydin. The shorter, more direct route from Muğla to Denizli has long difficult stretches of unmetalled road.

The limestone terraces of Pamukkale

The great limestone terraces on the hillside near the village of Pamukkale are one of Nature's marvels. Over the centuries numerous thermal springs rich in lime — calcium bicarbonate to be precise — have formed a wide band of milky white deposits, covering the 100 m slope in terraced formations resembling a petrified waterfall and encircling natural thermal pools. They are an unforgettable sight, especially at sunset when, beneath the changing colours of the sky, framed by oleander bushes in bloom and with a backdrop of tumbling hills, the chalk white cascades with their glistening pools turn to shades of pink.

If at all possible arrange to spend at least one night at Pamukkale. On the plateau immediately above the limestone terraces, where the hot springs flow from the ground, a number of motels have been built amongst the imposing ruins of ancient Hierapolis. Most have incorporated large thermal springs for bathing. The spring which forms the swimming pool of the Motel Pamukkale has been used for bathing since antiquity; fragments of Roman cornices and columns still lie on the bottom.

H The thermal springs with their blood-warm waters are a recognised form of treatment for rheumatism, neuralgia, and stomach, liver and kidney complaints. Patients drink the waters as well as bathing.

The attraction of Pamukkale is not only in its unique limestone cascades but also in the nearby ruins of Hierapolis.

Hierapolis. In Roman times, especially in the 2nd and 3rd centuries A.D., Hierapolis — situated just above the Pamukkale limestone terraces — was renowned for its thermal cures and its magnificent festivals and games; it was also an affluent city of herdsmen, wool dyers, weavers and merchants. Sad to say the uncontrolled encroachment of motels, camping places and shops onto this ancient site, aggravated by garish adverts and crudely installed electricity cables which must frustrate every photographer, largely deprive the extensive archaeological ruins of atmosphere. Low-flying jets screaming overhead from time to time also make it difficult for the visitor's thoughts to dwell on antiquity! Despite all this Hierapolis remains one of the best ancient sites in Asia Minor.

Of special interest are the (poorly reconstructed) Great Baths housing a library and a small museum; the ancient hot water spring at the Motel

Pamukkale nearby; and, also nearby, the ruins of a Byzantine church. Just beyond the motel and church are the remains of a long street, once flanked by arcades of shops, leading to the massive North Tower and on to the necropolis.

On the right of the arcaded street are the large ruins of a Roman bath, later converted into a Byzantine basilica (Hierapolis was an episcopal see until falling under Seljuk rule). The extensive necropolis contains numerous sarcophagi and tombs built by a variety of different peoples; among them are some strange circular structures possibly of Etruscan origin.

On the slope beyond the arcaded street stand the well-preserved Roman theatre and the 5th c. burial church of the Apostle Philip.

Aphrodisias is rather off the beaten track and relatively few people visit it, although it is actually well worth seeing. For those making their way from Kuşadası or Izmir to Pamukkale it involves a detour of either 66 km or 85 km, leaving the E 24 at or just beyond Nazilli and taking the road to Karacasu, continuing past Karacasu itself until the excavations of the Carian-Roman city are reached near the village of Geyre. Alternatively a round trip can be made, including visits to both ancient sites, by turning off at Nazilli for Geyre and Aphrodisias, then continuing via Tavas to Denizli and Pamukkale, returning to the coast on the E 24 from Denizli.

At the time of the Roman emperors Aphrodisias was famous for its fertility cult and for its school of medicine, sculpture and philosophy. Best preserved of its buildings are the theatre, the town walls, the large stadium (for 30,000 spectators), the Odeion, the thermal baths (dating from the time of Hadrian), and the ruins of a Temple of Aphrodite, later converted into a church, with its Ionic colonnade. The interesting museum possesses some fine sculptures.

Gathering olives in southern Anatolia

South Anatolian Coast

The southern coast of Turkey extends from Fethiye on the Aegean to the border with Syria south of Iskenderun. This coast, especially the stretch between Antalya and Alanya, is often referred to as the Turquoise Coast, or the Turkish Riviera. Borrowed from the Italian Riviera the latter name is appropriate, not only because the mountain chain which forms its backcloth resembles the Ligurian Alps, but also because of its lush vegetation bearing an astonishing abundance of blooms. Wild oleander grows luxuriantly, gardens and parks are full of flowers and flowering trees, and the land is chequered with orange and lemon groves, vineyards, fig and pomegranate and other varieties of tropical plant.

The coast between Fethiye and Antalya was for a long time very inaccessible, having been opened up only recently by construction of a new but twisting mountain road. This part of the coast, with its numerous small bays, islands and little-known ancient sites, is romantically wild and desolate, its attractions nowhere more evident than in the Bey Mountains where peaks rise to over 3000 metres. Running eastwards from Antalya is a narrow, extremely fertile coastal plain sheltered by the Taurus Mountains.

The coast between Fethiye and Kemer near Antalya, and to the east of Antalya, remains almost untouched by international tourism. It is dotted with small towns and villages visited only rarely by foreigners. In many places treasures from the past lie undiscovered in the earth and on the seabed, one day perhaps to grace a museum or enrich the landscape with an archaeological site.

Kaş Pop. 1500

Kaş lies in a picturesque bay encircled by mountains, at the most westerly point of the Turkish Mediterranean coast. Not long ago it was no more than a fishing village and haunt of sponge-divers. Now freshly painted and with new craft shops, tea-rooms, taverns and a modern marina it has been transformed into a pretty, peaceful, holiday resort. Stone

Xanthos

sarcophagi around the harbour and a Hellenistic theatre are an evocation of its ancient past.

🚌 **Xanthos,** built on a rocky outcrop on a hillside some 50 km to the north-west, was the capital of Lycia, and very probably the oldest republic in the world (having a system of popular representation and a president). The extensive remains of this sizeable ancient city date from the 6th c. B.C. to the 7th c. A.D. The monolithic pillar tombs with urn chambers, and parts of the town walls, are of Lycian origin. The theatre, temple and agora (market) are Greek and Roman, and the small churches are Byzantine.

On the way to Xanthos the road passes through the idyllic village of Kalkan with its little harbour, a carefully guarded secret amongst yachtsmen.

East of Kas is the largest necropolis on the south coast, with numerous sarcophagi; also the island of Kekov where there are remains of a Lycian city, partly on land and partly submerged beneath the sea.

South Anatolian Coast

Finike Pop. 1500

Finike, ancient Phoenicus, is a small town surrounded by orange groves with sandy beaches and a marina. About 6 km to the north-east near the excavated foundations of the ancient town of Limyra, the rocks are honeycombed with typical Lycian rock tombs. The scenery at the nearby Karagöl (Black Lake) is extraordinarily beautiful.

Demre (Myra). From the village of Kale between Finike and Kaş a road turns off to the small town of Demre. From there it is only about 2 km to the impressive ruins of ancient Myra. A restored Byzantine church contains the empty tomb of St Nicholas, who was a priest and later bishop here. Around December 6th each year festivities commemorating him are held at Myra. Legend has it that in the 4th c. A.D., in the village next to Myra, there lived a poor family with three daughters one of whom was to be sold into slavery to provide dowries for the other two. But on December 6th, before the girl was to be taken away, a bag of coins was tossed into the house. The same thing happened the following two years, till in the end all three daughters were able to marry. The priest Nicholas was later discovered to be the anonymous benefactor.

Kemer Pop. 1000

The fishing village of Kemer — 40 km south-west of Antalya — enjoys magnificent views of the Bey and Taurus Mountains. Among its other attractions are endless peaceful sandy beaches and large forested areas which invite walking. There are also ancient ruins not too far away. Kemer is a new resort still being developed, with several new hotels, holiday bungalows, guest houses and holiday clubs such as the Palmiya and the Milta; it offers a considerable range of leisure activities. A large new holiday apartment hotel has been built in Tekerlektepe Bay. There is

Demre (Myra)

also already a Club Mediterranée. A Robinson Club has been opened close to the ancient ruins of Phaselis with exceptionally pleasant grounds and buildings. It offers a variety of sports and entertainment. Further holiday accommodation is under construction.

Kiziltepe Camping Site

Phaselis (5 km to the south). The three harbour basins of this ancient port, founded by Greek settlers from Rhodes in the 7th c. B.C., are still recognizable. Also to be seen are the remains of houses on the harbour road, a theatre with a panoramic view of the mountains, the aqueduct and the necropolis. The still very unspoiled and tranquil excavation site concealed in a pine wood can be reached by boat or with ease on foot from the Robinson Club.

Ancient ruins. There are quite a number of Lycian, Greek and Roman ruins around Kemer. Most are difficult to get to and not particularly

impressive from an architectural point of view, but sites such as Korydalla, Rhodiapolis, Akalissos and Kormos in the mountains, and Olympos and Chimaera on the coast towards Finike are quite unspoiled and set in breathtaking scenery.

Chimaera was the home of the legendary fire-breathing monster with the body of a goat, a lion's head and the tail of a dragon. Burning natural gas escaping from a hole in the rock is thought most likely to have given rise to this legend.

For further interesting excursions see below under Antalya and following towns.

Antalya Pop. 180,000

Antalya is the provincial capital of a coastal and mountain province known in antiquity as Pamphylia, which clearly held great attractions for Greeks, Lydians, Persians and Romans. Founded in the 2nd c. B.C. by Attalos II, King of Pergamon, and named by him Attaleia, it is unquestionably one of the loveliest cities in Turkey. Framed by mountains and enthroned on a terrace above a wide bay, Antalya is dotted with parks and criss-crossed by alleys, and ablaze with the colour of exotic flowers and trees. After Kuşadasi its surroundings include more archaeological sites than any other town in western Turkey. Another of its attractions is the extremely pleasant climate, with mild winters and hot, almost rain-free summers relieved by refreshing mountain breezes. Not surprisingly tourism is growing faster in the area around Antalya and Alanya than anywhere else in the country, with more hotels and holiday accommodation being built.

The Old Town by the harbour and the ancient harbour itself are today a remarkable example of what is best in modern restoration and reconstruction. The marina and leisure centre

Yivli minaret

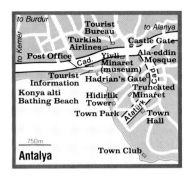

Antalya

to Burdur
to Kemer
to Alanya

Tourist Bureau
Turkish Airlines
Post Office
Castle Gate
Ala-eddin Mosque
Cad.
Yivli Minaret (museum)
Tourist Information
Hadrian's Gate
Konya alti Bathing Beach
Hidirlik Tower
Truncated Minaret
Town Park
Atatürk
Town Hall
750m
Town Club

incorporate old buildings, blending new with old by a return to traditional styles. The architects have avoided creating only an open-air museum-piece, successfully preserving the area's functional vitality. The leisure centre has an information bureau, various restaurants and cafés, a typical Turkish pudding shop (*muhallebici*), souvenir and craft shops, boutiques, a hotel modelled on an old-style rest-house but with modern comforts and facilities, and an open-air theatre built in the shape of an amphitheatre. As intended it is also a place where foreigner and Turk meet and mingle. There is a scheme in hand to restore more of the old Turkish houses in the Antalya Citadel.

Roman and Seljuk buildings

The Roman triumphal archway (partly restored) was erected in A.D. 130 to commemorate a visit by the Emperor Hadrian. The town walls, remains of which run along the Atatürk Boulevard and round the harbour, were built by the Romans on Greek foundations and later extended by the Seljuks. The truncated Minaret (Kisik Minare) incorporates the remains of more ancient buildings. Among the earliest examples of Seljuk architecture are the 13th c. Karatay Medrese (Koranic School) with an elaborate portal, and the 13th c. Yivli Mosque, with its fluted minaret (Yivli

Minare) decorated with blue-green tiles. The mosque and its associated buildings now contain a large folk museum. Definitely not to be missed is the Archaeological Museum on the road leading to Kemer, with exhibits from Perge, Aspendos, Side, Termessos, Myra and other ancient sites. As well as the Yivli Minarct, Antalya's other main landmark is the Hidirlik Kulesi Tower (probably a converted lighthouse), which offers a fine vista of the town and harbour.

 There are several flights daily between Antalya and Istanbul and Ankara. Holiday flights to Alanya, Incekum and Side also serve Antalya. Turkish shipping lines run services from Istanbul and Izmir to ports as far south as Iskenderun.

There is a pebble and sand beach 4 km west near the new commercial harbour at Konyaalti; 12 km east of Antalya is the very spacious *Lara* beach.

 In several hotels.

Several hamams.

Especially in the bazaar, at the old harbour and in the town park.

In several hotels.

Several hotels and discothèques.

From time to time during the holiday season.

Several, sometimes with belly-dancing.

In the Hastahane Caddesi, in the bazaar and at the old harbour.

 Kiziltepe Camping on the way to Kemer and *Bambus Camping* on the way to Lara beach.

Waterfalls, mountains and ancient sites

Excursions with the accent on scenery: by boat to the lower Düden Falls which plunge over vertical cliffs into the sea near Antalya, or by bus or car to the upper Düden Falls, 11 km inland; also into the mountains with their Aleppo pines, holm-oaks, cedars and sweet-smelling macchia, or by boat along the rugged coast towards Kemer and Finike. Some 25 km north to the Karain cave where there are stone-age remains and drawings scratched into the rock.

Easily reached from Antalya are the outstanding ancient sites at Termessos (30 km north-west) and, to the east, Perge (18 km), Aspendos (40 km) and Side (75 km).

Termessos. The very ancient fortress-city of Termessos, built by Pisidian mountain tribes, enjoys an unparalleled vista over the Gulf of Antalya. Virtually inaccessible and heavily fortified, the town escaped attack by Alexander the Great in 334 B.C. It reached the peak of its prosperity in the 2nd to 1st centuries B.C. and was abandoned by its inhabitants in late Roman times following an earthquake.

The site is still in process of excavation but there are nevertheless a number of very interesting ruins in evidence, the most impressive being the theatre, the agora, a colonnaded street, parts of the encircling walls, the necropolis, aqueduct and cisterns.

Perge, one of the principal cities of Pamphylia, prospered under the patronage of many Roman emperors and was one of the first Christian communities in Asia Minor; it was here that the Apostle Paul is believed to have preached for the first time. The ruins are extensive and it is best to concentrate on the Roman town gate flanked by two round towers, the still earlier colonnaded street with its numerous columns, the large, well-preserved stadium, the agora, the Roman baths and the theatre built into the hillside.

Roman ruins, Perge

Aspendos theatre

At Side

Aspendos boasts one of the best-preserved theatres to have survived from antiquity (built by the Romans in the 2nd c. A.D. on the site of a still older theatre). The stage building is almost perfectly preserved, lacking only its marble facing and the statues in the niches. The acoustics are exceptional, largely a result of the shell-like curvature of the seating. With some 15,000 places the theatre is used for concerts, plays and folk dancing and music during the Antalya Festival in late May and early June.

In the acropolis on the hilltop there are remains of the agora, town fortifications and an aqueduct.

Side Pop. 1000

The small town of Side (pronounced See-day) is beautifully sited in a wide bay surrounded by orange groves and cotton fields. Only a few years ago it was no more than a tiny fishing village. Now it is rapidly becoming one of the busiest holiday resorts on Turkey's southern coast, already possessing several modern hotels, motels and holiday apartments, and sports and entertainment facilities. Spacious holiday centres and clubs have been built on both sides of the town.

 Ancient Side

The extensive excavations of ancient Side, an important trading centre and slave market in Hellenistic and Byzantine times, lie close by the modern town.

With seating for an audience of almost 17,000 its theatre was the largest in Pamphylia. From the upper rows there are superb views of the ancient ruins and the sea. The most important structures, dating mainly from the 2nd and 3rd centuries A.D., are the victory monument, the agora, the town wall (which still has some of its towers), the main gateway, and the remains of a 30-km-long aqueduct which brought water from the Taurus Mountains. The small museum housed in the Roman Baths has two exceptionally fine sarcophagi and some equally fine Roman heads (heads were something of a forte of Roman sculptors, often appearing on monuments). Parts of the ancient town are sadly overgrown or covered with sand from the dunes.

 On both sides of the town there are long, wide and largely flat sandy beaches very suitable for children.

   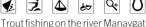

 Trout fishing on the river Manavgat as well as sea fishing.

 Several restaurants around the harbour.

 Sometimes in the Hotel *Cennet.*

 Souvenir shops and boutiques on the harbour front.

 Fethi Camping, and at the Hotel *Sorgun* (4 km along the road towards Manavgat).

 To Manavgat (Pop. 7000), a small town 8 km inland. A bazaar, tea-rooms, coffee-houses and typical little restaurants full of local atmosphere, enhanced by its great popularity with Turkish visitors.

To a low but wide waterfall on the river Manavgat 14 km from Side, where there is a pleasant restaurant, tea-garden and welcome shade.

For further excursions see under Antalya.

70 km to Alanya.

Incekum

This small seaside resort with a number of modest, middle-priced hotels has a lovely sandy beach surrounded by cliffs, rocks and green hills. There is a bus service to Alanya, 22 km away. The coast road by-passes the holiday accommodation which is right on the beach.

 Flat beach with fine sand suitable for children.

Alanya Fortress and harbour

 In the Hotel *Alara.*

   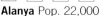

Alanya Pop. 22,000

Alanya is still the most popular holiday resort on the 'Turkish Riviera'. In the future Kemer and Side may come to offer more in the way of tourist accommodation and facilities, but they cannot compete with Alanya's magnificent scenery, its architecture and beaches, and its grottos with a reputation for healing. The high Taurus Mountains contrast wonderfully with the flat sandy beaches while between the mountains and the coast banana plantations, orange and lemon groves and palms more than satisfy any European desire for southern luxuriance.

On its rocky promontory jutting out into the sea, the almost perfectly-preserved Seljuk fortress encloses within its triple walls the narrow alleys of the Old Town, which has a romantic oriental atmosphere which will delight the visitor.

Alanya's most famous visitors, Anthony and Cleopatra, came here on honeymoon about 2000 years ago.

 The fortress

From pre-Christian times until the Middle Ages Alanya was a pirate stronghold. Pompey destroyed the pirate's fortress in 67 B.C. and it was not until the 13th c. that the Sultan Alâeddin Keykubat built another, even larger and stronger. The fortress walls, courtyards, walled passages and gates are all impressive and highly photogenic. From the vantage point of a platform on the walls of the Citadel (250 m above sea-level) there is a breathtaking panoramic view. This is a place with a grisly past, however. In Seljuk times, having been held without food and water for three days, prisoners were made to hurl three stones down into the sea. Those who succeeded were spared and recruited into the army, but the unfortunates who failed were themselves thrown from the walls.

Near the entrance to the courtyard of the inner citadel there is a small Byzantine church (traces of frescos) and next to it the deepest of some 400 cisterns in the fortress. Within the outer fortress wall on the side facing the present town are the remains of the old Seljuk city with small mosques, a caravanserai and a covered bazaar.

The dockyard. Keykubat also had a dockyard constructed and joined to the fortress. The dockyard building, hewn out of the rock, is still in use after 700 years. The free-standing octagonal Red Tower, so called on account of its brickwork, was built by the Sultan's architect from Aleppo for the protection of the yard.

The Archaeological Museum is small but has some interesting finds from the Alanya area.

 The Damlatas Cave, at the foot of the cliffs on the landward end of the promontory, was discovered only in 1948. It has splendid stalactites and stalagmites, and with a constant temperature of 22–23°C and an unusually high carbon-dioxide content in its air, is renowned for the relief it brings to sufferers from asthma and bronchitis. Other caves, which have mysterious light effects but no claim to healing qualities, can only be reached by boat; of these the Blue Grotto and Maiden Grotto are the most visited.

 East and west of the promontory there are large expanses of fine sand.

 The flat, spacious beach is ideal for children. While there is no playground and nothing organised specially for children, the smaller ones can play happily in the sand and the older ones will enjoy the camel rides, boat trips and visits to the grottos and fortress.

 At the harbour.

 From the steep slopes of the promontory.

 If you can find a speedboat available.

 At the *Alantur, Panorama* and *Banana* Motels.

 At the *Alantur* Motel and *Yeni* Motel International.

 In the larger motels (also speciality menus).

In the Old Town.

In the *Alantur, Banana* and *Merhaba* motels; also at *'La Bohème'* and in the very stylish and lovely old *Hani Sarapsa* caravanserai (15 km away).

There is a performance every week in one of the motels; also at the weekly barbecue parties held during the summer season.

Anamur castle

English books are sold in the Pamfilya travel agency. In early and late season, when rain occasionally falls, the agency organises cookery classes in Turkish specialities.

Colourful, handwoven silk shawls and scarves (in many houses in the Old Town women can be seen working at looms which have been used for generations); embroideries, leather goods, carpets, copperwork, and painted bottle-gourds (*cala-basses*). Expect to be pressed to buy handwoven textiles, especially at the entrance to the fortress.

Organised day excursions to Antalya calling at Termessos; to the Manavgat Falls; to Side, Aspendos, Perge and Anamur; two-day tours to Pammukale; tours lasting several days to Cappadocia.

Beginning south-east of Alanya is a stretch of coastline delightful for its scenery and rich in its culture but as yet largely neglected by package tours.

It is a very worthwhile destination for the more adventurous independent traveller. Even here road conditions and accommodation have improved considerably in recent years.

Anamur Pop. 12,000

Despite its location at the southernmost point of Mediterranean Turkey (on roughly the same latitude as the southern tip of Sicily), and despite its lovely beach (but with only a small motel), Anamur would be of little tourist interest were it not for ancient Anamurion only 9 km to the west and the even greater attraction of Mamuriye Kalesi, the fortress of Anamur, 7 km to the east.

During the Middle Ages the fortified castle, built above Roman foundations on a rocky tongue-shaped headland, was one of the most feared pirate strongholds in the eastern Mediterranean. With its apertureless walls and over 30 round or square towers, it is now one of the best-preserved fortresses in Turkey. Occasionally folk festivals are held there.

Pompeiopolis from Mersin

At the ancient city of Anamurion the most impressive remains are those of the Byzantine city walls with their defence towers and the two theatre complexes which provide glorious sea views.

Silifke Pop. 15,000

Founded in 300 B.C. the small town of Silifke stands on the right bank of the river Göksu (river Kalykadnos in antiquity and until the Middle Ages), close to its delta. The Byzantines and the Lesser Armenians came into bitter conflict over Silifke. In later years it was taken by the Venetians who used it as a harbour until it finally fell into Ottoman hands.

The town is dominated by the extensive ruins of a fortress said to have been built partly by the Knights of the Order of St John and partly by the Armenians.

The coastal area between Silifke and Mersin (95 km to the east) is dotted with the ruins of ancient small towns and old fortresses. About 20 km east of Silifke are the remains of a Roman bath with a mosaic of the 'Three Graces bathing' and, 3 km inland, the so-called Vale of Paradise (Cennet Deresi), a karst gorge with an intriguing grotto. Korykos, further towards Mersin, was once a Roman-Byzantine settlement and later a pirates' haven; as well as good sandy beaches there are ruins of a land fortress and a second fortress, Kiz Kalesi, on the islet offshore. About half-way to Mersin at Kanlidivane is the necropolis of ancient Kanytelis with tombs and sarcophagi and the ruins of a Byzantine church. At Mut, 75 km north of Silifke on the road to Konya, are the remains of a large Ottoman fortress and two 14th c. mosques. There is a hydrofoil service from Tasuku 4 km west of Silifke to Girne (formerly Kyrenia) in the Turkish part of Cyprus.

Mersin Pop. 200,000

Mersin is Turkey's principal south coast port, a modern industrial city with oil refineries. Located on the edge of the exceptionally fertile Cilician plain (called Çukurova) of which Adana is the centre, the processing and export of tropical

Tarsus

fruit, tobacco and cotton figure large in the city's economy. There are some good new hotels, and Mersin is worth considering as a base for exploring the eastern Mediterranean coast. In the autumn Turkoman nomads move down from the high valleys of the Taurus Mountains to winter on the milder coastal plain, pitching their tents in the areas around the city.

🚌 To Tarsus (25 km to the east) birthplace of the Apostle Paul. Cicero was governor here in Roman times, and it is said that Cleopatra and Mark Anthony first met here. Of the ancient town buried in the hillside only the scant remains of a gate and temple have been uncovered.

There is a ferry from Mersin to Magosa (formerly Famagusta) in Cyprus.

Adana Pop. 500,000

The provincial capital Adana lies on the river Seyhan — a dam upstream provides facilities for bathing and boating — in the middle of the large Çukurova plain from which it derives its wealth. It is the most important industrial city in southern Turkey (several hotels of various categories) but can still boast a typically oriental Old Town.

📷 Dating from the Ottoman period are the covered bazaar, the 16th c. Great Mosque (Ulu Cami), the Ramazanoğlu Mosque (14th c.) and Akça Mescit prayer house (15th c.) which clearly display the influence of neighbouring Syria. There is an impressive 300-m-long stone bridge which still has 14 of its original 21 arches. Also worth seeing is the regional museum; the ethnographic and archaeological section contains, among other items, a small Hittite statue made of crystal and a richly ornamented Roman sarcophagus.

🚌 Misis, Anazarbus and Karatepe

To the excavation site of Misis, 25 km east, near Yakapinar on the river Ceyhan which flows parallel to the Seyhan; there is a small museum with good figurative mosaics from the 3rd and 4th centuries A.D.

To Anazarbus, 85 km from Adana, turning north off the E 5 near the town of Ceyhan (with its nearby hill fortress Yilan Kalesi and a Hittite rock relief). The road branching off leads to Ayşehoca and Çukurköpru, not far from which is the site of ancient Anazarbus where there are numerous and substantial remains from the Roman,

Byzantine and Armenian periods.

At Kadirli beyond Anazarbus (125 km from Adana) a poor road leads to the very interesting late Hittite settlement of Karatepe (about 9th c. B.C.), situated in what is now a national park by the river Ceyhan. There is an open-air museum which includes ancient inscriptions and stone reliefs, and the remains of a fortress etc.

Iskenderun Pop. 100,000

In the south-east corner of the Çukurova plain, at the foot of the Nur Dağlari mountain chain (2262 m, also called the Amanos Mountains) is the port of Iskenderun, founded by Alexander the Great but now a modern city. It is an important naval and commercial port and the last stop for Turkish passenger-line ferries from Istanbul. Thanks to the subtropical climate there are delightful parks, gardens with tea-rooms and a pleasant seafront promenade. The town was ceded to Syria in 1918 but restored to Turkey in 1939.

8 km south to the Belen Pass (750 m with magnificent views) where there is a Crusader fortress.

To the site of the battle of Issos, 40 km to the north near the village of Dört Yol (with a tower, covered bazaar, hamam and mosque dating from the Ottoman period). Here in 333 B.C. Alexander the Great completely destroyed the Persian army under Darius III. A medieval fortress, Toprakkale, commands the narrow entry to the plain of Issos.

Hatay Pop. 90,000

Hatay, sometimes still called Antakya, is the provincial capital of the south-east province of Hatay. It lies in the foothills of the Amanos Mountains, on the edge of the fertile Amik plain, 30 km from the sea and 60 km from the Syrian frontier. A substantial proportion of the population is of Arab descent. The colourful, noisy bazaar, heavy with aromas of the orient, should not be missed.

 Hatay is the Antioch mentioned in the Bible, and in the 2nd c. B.C. had half a million inhabitants. It was an important trading and cultural centre and played a major role in the conversion of Anatolia to Christianity. Its first Christian community is said to have been established by the Apostle Paul in a grotto, 2 km from the town, where there is now a pilgrim chapel.

The main attraction is the Archaeological Museum which has an outstanding collection of 2nd to 4th c. A.D. mosaics from the villas of Antioch and nearby Daphni. The mosaics have mythical and Christian motifs. It was in the lovely laurel and cypress grove at Daphni that, according to the legend, the nymph Daphne escaped the advances of Apollo by being transformed into a laurel tree.

Also of interest in Hatay are the remains of a Roman aqueduct, some remnants of the originally many-towered town walls, the citadel on its rock plateau and the Habib Neccar Mosque which was once a Byzantine church.

15 km to the south is the ruined Crusader fortress of Kürşat.

Mosaic from the museum at Hatay

Mevlana Mausoleum, Konya

Central Anatolia

In reality the so-called Central Anatolian Plateau is not so central, since the eastern Anatolian highlands (not dealt with in this guide) extend westwards across almost half of Turkey. Nor, when a relief map is studied, does the term 'plateau' seem particularly appropriate. The base level of this upland region — little more than a wilderness in parts — is generally about 1000 m, dropping to about 900 m in depressions near Ankara and the great salt lake Tuz Gölü. Yet at numerous points the 'plateau' rises to heights of between 1300 and 1700 m, and mountains of over 2000 m are not uncommon around the rim.

At their centre these uplands have little to offer the tourist; the areas around the periphery on the other hand are scenically very attractive with a wealth of things to see. To the south-west are many lakes and mountains in the triangle of country between Burdur, Afyon and Konya; around Ankara there is an interesting area rich in cultural history; but above all else, on the south-eastern edge of the plateau, there is the unique tuff landscape of Cappadocia, with its 'fairy chimneys', its ancient underground cities, its rock dwellings and richly painted rock churches.

Burdur Alt. 975 m; Pop. 40,000

Burdur and the neighbouring Isparta lie on the two shortest and best roads from Antalya via Afyon to Ankara or Istanbul. Burdur is barely a kilometre from the large, sulphurous Burdur salt lake with its richly varied birdlife. The lake also offers facilities for water-sports. Close to the south shore of the lake an 8000-year-

old settlement was discovered at Hacilar. Ceramics and other prehistoric finds from the site can be seen in the small museum at Burdur. The town's main mosque dates from the 14th c.

🚌 12 km south of Burdur to the stalactite- and stalagmite-filled Insuyu grotto through which a river flows.

In the wider vicinity of Burdur there are numerous fresh water lakes.

Afyon Alt. 1075 m; Pop. 50,000

Afyon has been an important crossroads since the earliest times. Not so long ago it was the caravan routes which met here; now it is the main roads from Izmir, Ephesus, Antalya, Konya, Ankara and Istanbul. The town is surrounded by poppy fields, opium being produced under state regulation. 'Afyon' is the Turkish word for opium.

The high, brooding, rocky fortress hill, up which climb the houses of the Old Town, is the most distinctive feature of what is otherwise a modern provincial capital. In Afyon itself the Fountain Mosque (Kuyulu Camii) with its beautiful minaret, the Great Mosque (Ulu Cami), a typical Seljuk wooden Mosque dating from the 13th c., the 15th c. Gedik Ahmet Paşa Medrese which houses a folk museum, and the very old fortress ruins (lovely distant views), are all worth seeing. The archaeological museum has a collection of finds from the area, dating from the Stone Age to the Byzantine period.

North of Afyon

Near Ihsaniye (35 km north of Afyon) are the remarkable Aslantaş and Aslankaya rock tombs (not always easy to find). Dating from the Greek and Phrygian periods — 6th to 5th c. B.C. — the geometric decoration, Phrygian characters and recurrent lion figures are highly distinctive. The tombs are reached via narrow, and in places poor, roads.

At Aizani on the Gediz road (the best route from Afyon is via Kütahya) there is a reasonably well-preserved Temple of Jupiter built in the time of the Emperor Hadrian. Its columns are mounted on Asiatic-style bases and crowned with Ionic and Corinthian capitals.

Near Kirka, about 40 km due north of Afyon, lies Midas Şehri, the city of Midas. Here, behind façades hewn in the rock

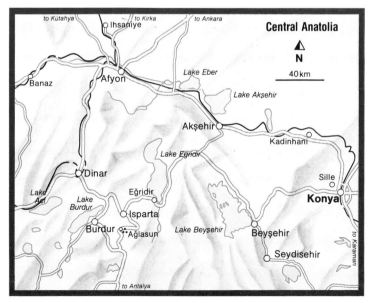

are a number of small cult sanctuaries. The most impressive is known as the Tomb of Midas — though its authenticity has now been disproved — the façade being decorated with some especially fine carvings.

50 km beyond Kirka, the town of Seyitgazi is the site of a mighty Dervish monastery, still well-preserved. A cenotaph high on a hill here is visible from miles away.

The former Phrygian capital of Gordion is reached via the E 23 Afyon to Ankara road (see page 88).

Isparta Alt. 1035 m; Pop. 65,000

Isparta is a centre of rose-growing and manufacture of hand-knotted carpets. The carpets, primarily of the sort for everyday use, are traded at the morning carpet market (daily until about 11 a.m.) Small ovens to be seen on the outskirts of the town are used in the production of attar of roses, everywhere on sale here. The town's small museum is mainly devoted to carpet production, but also has some exhibits from the Roman period.

To Ağlasun, 40 km south, to the ruins of the Hellenistic-Roman town of Sagalassos (1700 m) which include a temple with Corinthian columns, a theatre and rock tombs.

Anyone driving from Antalya to Cappadocia via Konya should take the route north from Antalya, through Ağlasun and Isparta. Until Beyşehir is reached, the alternative route which turns north beyond Manavgat to Akseki and then Konya, shown on some maps as a through road, is in places only fit for vehicles (and drivers!) equipped for crossing mountains and rough terrain.

Eğridir on Lake Eğridir
Alt. 920 m; Pop. 7000

The large and beautiful emerald green Lake Eğridir is now a National Park. Like Lake Balaton in Hungary it is extremely shallow; the water is perfectly clear. There are small sandy beaches along its wooded shores, and no mosquitoes.

Eğridir is known all over the world for its freshwater lobsters. The annual catch of some 15,000 tons is mostly exported (even to Canada).

There is only one town on the 517 sq. km lake, the extremely picturesque Eğridir, its little harbour overlooked by the still impressive ruins of a Seljuk fortress. Its Hizirbey Mosque, built above an arch, boasts the only minaret in the world under which a road passes, and the 13th c. Dündar Bey Medrese opposite has a fine portal.

 On both sides of the town.

 In the National Park.

 In the town and by the lake.

Beyşehir Alt. 1150 m; Pop. 9000

Beyşehir lies some 95 km south-east of Konya on a lake of the same name (grand mountain scenery, and a rich variety of waterfowl). The town makes a good stopping place on the way from Antalya or Alanya to Konya. It has a pleasant lakeside promenade and restaurant, a lively market, the wooden Seljuk Eşrefoğlu Mosque (13th c., with türbe and medrese), and, on the other side of the little waterway, a former Dervish monastery.

Konya Alt. 1027 m; Pop. 300,000

Konya was both the capital and the religious centre of the medieval Seljuk Empire. Richly endowed with art treasures and vibrant with a typically Turkish-oriental atmosphere, Islamic traditions are also stronger here than in other western Anatolian cities (on certain days, for example, no alcohol is available, and in many restaurants none is served). Konya is situated in an area of great scenic beauty on the southern edge of the Anatolian plateau, flanked on two sides by foothills of the Taurus Mountains. The countryside around the town has many interesting places.

Town of the Whirling Dervishes

Legend has it that Konya was the first town to reappear from the waters of the Flood. Be that as it may, there are certainly traces of human settlement here which date back to the 3rd millennium B.C. It was only under the rule of the Seljuk sultans, Alâeddin Keykubat in particular, that the city achieved major importance, however.

The order of Whirling Dervishes (*Mevlevi Dervishes*), founded in Konya about 1225 by the poet and mystic Celaleddin Rumi (known as Mevlâna or 'our guide'), became very influential in the Ottoman Empire. The name derived from their whirling ritual dances, performed to music, during which the Dervishes attained an ecstatic state of trance. The Mevlevi were highly esteemed as interpreters of the Koran and also as fanatical warriors. Although the order was dissolved by Atatürk it still has many followers and Mevlâna is still revered.

Museums and Mosques

Citadel Hill. As well as offering the finest view of the city, Alâeddin Park on Citadel Hill also contains the ruins of a Seljuk palace, and the famous Alâeddin Mosque. The restored mosque has 42 columns with Roman and Byzantine capitals and a superbly carved minbar and mihrab. At the foot of the hill are the 13th c. Karatay Medrese with a small but interesting ceramics museum, and the Ince Minare Medrese (with an elaborate portal) which houses a collection of stone and wood carvings. South of the citadel is the tiled Sirçali Medrese, now the Museum of Islamic Gravestones, and beyond it the mosque, tomb and baths of the Sahib Ata (the mosque has a beautifully carved door). Close by is the small Archaeological Museum (open daily, afternoons only on Monday and Tuesday) with Roman and Byzantine finds among its exhibits (statues,

Whirling Dervishes, Konya

sarcophagi and glasses etc.) Konya also has a small ethnographic museum.

Mevlâna Müzesi, the monastery of the Whirling Dervishes — now a museum — is the jewel in Konya's crown. As well as the gold embroidered drapes and strange Dervish head-dresses adorning the sarcophagi of the order's founder Mevlâna and his followers, the monastery's treasures also include priceless old Anatolian carpets, valuable brocades, Koranic manuscripts and prayer desks, ancient musical instruments, and manuscripts of Rumi's poems.

Both the Mevlâna Müzesi, with its very typical green conical türbe, and the nearby Selim Mosque (beautiful main entrance and interior) are always crowded. Both too are highly photogenic and there is an excellent view of the monastery from the open space behind.

 Festival of the Whirling Dervishes, December 15th to 17th.

Decorated portal, Ince Minare Medrese, Konya

Especially on Alâeddin Boulevard; good food also in the Hotel *Saray*.

 Konya is famous for its carpets. The main shopping streets are the Alâeddin Boulevard and Mevlâna Caddesi; just to the south are the bazaar and Aziziye Camii (with unusually ornate minarets).

Around Konya

Meram, 8 km, a delightful little place with vineyards.

Sille, 10 km (two rock churches with pieces of fresco).

Catal Höyük, 40 km to the south. Excavations on this site uncovered, 20 m below the surface, a settlement dating from about 6700 B.C. with shrines, dwellings and workshops. Most of the prehistoric finds are now in the Archaeological Museum in Ankara.

Karaman, 100 km south-east, a small town with a citadel (partly 12th c.) and several old mosques. The mosque of the Ak Tekke Monastery (14th c.) contains the tomb of Mevlâna's mother. It was from Karaman in the 13th c. that the Turkoman Karamanoğlu tribe established Turkish as the official language in large parts of Anatolia, in place of the Persian used by the Seljuks.

Akşehir, 130 km north-west of Konya, birthplace of Nasreddin Hoça, the 13th c. Turkish humorist and teller of folk tales (a festival is held commemorating him in the first half of July); there are mosques dating from the 13th to 16th centuries, partly restored in the 19th c.

Aksaray Alt. 1100 m; Pop. 30,000

A small village about 100 km from Konya on the road to Aksaray is still the site of the early 13th c. Seljuk caravanserai Sultan Hani. The richly ornamented gateway, the encircling wall, the stabling, living quarters and kitchens, store and small pillared chapel which doubled as a look-out, have all been beautifully restored. At one time similar fortress-like caravanserais, of which a number have survived, especially in central Anatolia, were to be found every 40 to 50 km along the caravan routes, roughly the distance covered in a day by a camel caravan.

Further along the road across the steppe the extinct Hasan volcano, 2965 m high, comes into view, rising up from the plateau which at this point is about 1100 m above sea level.

The town of Aksaray itself is a green oasis in the midst of the barren steppe. Its 14th and 15th c. mosques and medreses and its Hotel *Orhan Ağaçli* which offers good accommodation (camping site and swimming pool), make Aksaray a worthwhile place to break a journey, particularly as it stands at the gateway to Cappadocia.

 The extraordinary tuff landscape begins only 11 km east of Aksaray. Branching off to the south is the seldom-visited Melendiz valley where, scattered over an area of 10 km between the little towns of Belisirma and Ihlara, are seven rock churches, each with paintings in different styles, but all very fine examples. The Seljuk caravanserai Ağzikara Han, on the main road from Aksaray to Nevşehir, has a most beautiful stalactitic portal.

Cappadocia

The Cappadocian landscape is unquestionably one of the great natural wonders of the world. About 3 million years ago, powerful eruptions from volcanos, including the now extinct and snow-covered Erciyes Dağı (3916 m) near Kayseri — visible from afar — covered the entire area between Aksaray and Ürgüp, Avanos and Niğde with vast quantities of ash and tuff. At the same time as innumerable water channels, most of which later dried out, were cutting into the gradually hardening layers, water and wind erosion formed thousand upon thousand of cones, pyramids, arches, and puckered ridges of folded rock. As they weathered, the towers and cones became more and more pointed and on many — the 'fairy chimneys' — a layer of harder stone has remained capping them like mushrooms. Oxidation has decked this strange fantasy world of nature in colour, sometimes muted, sometimes vivid, sometimes in cold shades and sometimes in warm. In spring flowers and greenery blossom in the hollows between the rocks.

Dwellings had already been carved out of the soft tuff as early as the Bronze Age, but between the 3rd and 13th centuries, underground cities, rock villages, hermitages, monasteries and literally hundreds of rock-hewn churches appeared. First and foremost it was here that Christians sought refuge from persecution by the Romans, and later by the insurgent Asiatic tribes seeking a foothold in Anatolia. Hermits and all manner of sects also came here in search of seclusion. Not simply rock chambers but also beds, chairs and tables were chiselled out of the tuff. The churches are magnificently painted, the stylistic emphasis shifting from the more ornamental to the more figurative in accordance with the prevalent ideas and sensibilities of the inhabitants at the time. Also discernible is the influence of the different peoples who ruled the area, from the Greeks, Romans and Byzantines, to the Persians, Seljuks, Mongols and Ottomans.

A great many of these early dwellings and rock churches can be visited, though a number are either temporarily or partly closed in the interests of preservation. Others are so off the beaten track as to be rarely come upon by strangers. Some rock dwellings are still inhabited, others have been turned into small shops, restaurants and even discothèques.

Nevşehir Alt. 1250 m; Pop. 40,000

Nevşehir is the provincial capital; it did not acquire importance until the 18th c. from which time the Kurşunlu Mosque with its medrese, charity kitchen and library also date. With several hotels it provides a base for exploration of the Cappadocian tuff and cave area.

 Chief among the attractions to be visited from Nevşehir are the

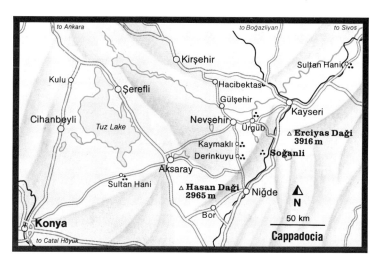

underground cities of Kaymakli and Derinkuyu, 20 km and 30 km south respectively, open to the public only in part. Seven or eight storeys deep they have good water supplies and ingenious ventilation systems. Chapels, assembly rooms and niches for sleeping are all provided for in an underground network of caves, passages and shafts which also contains grain stores, millstones and wine presses. Each storey can be individually barricaded off with stone slabs hewn from the rock, impossible to move from the outside. These sanctuaries were enlarged to their greatest capacity in the 11th and 12th centuries. In times of danger it is likely that several thousand people lived in them.

15 km north of Nevşehir there is a monks' colony carved out of the tuff, and at Gülşehir, 20 km north, fascinating and colourful rock formations as well as two rock churches (Karşi Kilise). At Hacibektaş, 30 km further on, there are onyx workshops and a Dervish monastery with the türbe of the 13th c. mystic Haci Bektaş.

Ürgüp Alt. 1200 m; Pop. 15,000

Ürgüp lies on the road from Nevşehir to Kayseri, at the foot of a steep flat-topped mountain honeycombed with rock dwellings. With hotels, bungalow parks, a camping site, small restaurants, several wine cellars and numerous carpet and souvenir shops it has become Cappadocia's tourist centre. It provides a good point of departure for visits to the particularly interesting nearby rock tombs and tuff formations of Göreme, Avcilar, Uchisar, Çavuşin and Zelve, as well as for the Soğanli Dere gorge, 50 km away.

Ortahisar, (7 km south-west of Ürgüp). Surrounded by bizarre rock formations produced by erosion, this highly photogenic little town clusters around a steep rock tower. The climb up to the caves needs care as the rock is both crumbly and slippery.

Göreme (7 km north-west of Ürgüp). Being one of the most accessible, this complex of rock churches and monasteries is also one of the most visited. The majority of the little churches are cruciform, many having the central dome supported by four columns carved out of the rock. Most date from the 10th to 13th centuries and almost all are decorated with magnificent and astonishingly well-preserved frescoes. They have names deriving from their decorative motifs or other distinguishing features: the 'Church of the Apple', the 'Church of the Sandals' (on account of two foot-prints), the 'Church of the Snakes', the 'Dark Church' etc. The largest, the 'Church of the Buckle' (Tokali Kilise), is decorated with scenes from the New Testament in chronological order, and over a hundred paintings of saints.

Avcilar (2 km west of Göreme) should certainly be visited for its five rock churches, but more especially in order to take a walk through the village itself where people still live in some of the striking rock cones. Onyx is also worked and sold here. Nearby (and elsewhere) there are unusual mushroom-shaped rock cones, their dark brown 'caps' contrasting with the paler 'stalks'.

Uchisar, (4 km west of Avcilar). The dwellings of this little town crowd over and around a massive rock, providing an

Above: 'Church of the Apple'.
Left and below: The rock churches and
monasteries at Göreme

Tuff region

to Ozkonak

N
10 km

Avanos
Zelve
Çavuşin
Avcilar
Üchisar
Göreme
Nevşehir
Ortahisar
Ürgüb
Kaymaklı
Derinkuyu
Mavrucan

enthralling view of the tuff landscape. To appreciate the fascinating houses, caves, crannies and rock formations to the full it is well worth walking at least some of the way to the upper town high on the rock.

Çavuşin (5 km north of Avcilar). There is much to see at Çavuşin and adequate time needs to be allowed for a visit. Amongst a group of caves in a steep, partly overhanging cliff is what is probably the oldest church in the entire area, dedicated to St John the Baptist. A short distance from the village, in a seldom visited but delightful cultivated area, are Güllü Dere ('the pink valley') and Kizil Cukur ('the red gorge'); in both there are rock hermitages and chapels with well-preserved paintings, probably dating from the time of the iconoclastic persecutions.

In Çavuşin itself there is a pretty restaurant in the rock (it has a mill on its sign) where thin pitta bread is baked in the open.

Zelve (3 km off the road from Avcilar to Avanos; 7 km north-east of Çavuşin). Spreading out in the shape of a fan the three valleys here provide some of the most striking scenery of Cappadocia's

rock and cave landscape. In one of the valleys the cave dwellings were still inhabited as recently as 1956 when the danger of rock falls caused their abandonment, which is why an Islamic prayer house is to be found among the Christian chapels. In one of the other valleys some of the chapels only have simple symbolic paintings by way of decoration.

Avanos (7km north of Çavuşin) is also known as the 'town on the red river'. As well as its many pottery workshops, onyx-ware and carpets are made and sold here too. At Özkonak, 20 km to the north-west, what is thought to be the largest of all the underground cities has now been opened to the public.

Mavrucan and Soğanli (30 to 50 km south of Ürgüp). There are more than 50 churches, large chambers and tombs hewn out of the tuff cones and rock face, with frescoes dating from the 9th to the 13th c. The road to the caves is rather poor in places.

Kayseri Alt. 1050 m; Pop. 250,000

Kayseri is the largest provincial centre on the eastern edge of the Anatolian plateau. Three factors in particular make it one of the cities in Turkey most worth seeing: its location at the foot of the usually snow-covered Erciyes Daği (3916 m), the highest mountain in central Anatolia; its many well-preserved buildings dating from the heyday of the Seljuk Empire in the 13th c.; and the genuineness of the vibrant oriental atmosphere of its Old Town behind the citadel.

As the principal town in the area Kayseri, or Eusebeia as it was then known, was already of some importance in the Hellenistic period. It later became capital of the Roman province of Cappadocia, its name being changed to Caesarea by Tiberius. It was from here in the 3rd c. A.D. that the conversion of Armenia to Christianity was first undertaken.

Wool traders, Kayseri

📷 The Old Town and the Citadel

Impressions of Kayseri today are inevitably dominated by the great Seljuk citadel, mosques, medreses and tombs (türbes), most dating from the first half of the 13th c. Of the three major fortified cities in the Seljuk Empire, Konya, Sivas and Kayseri, this was the largest and the mightiest (built between 1212 and 1236 and extended in the 15th c.); and only here has the citadel survived largely intact. Within its precincts are a marketplace and the 14th c. Fatih Mosque, while a climb on to the fortified walls is rewarded with an excellent view over the environs of the Old Town. In front of the citadel are the fortress-like 13th c. Honat Hatun Mosque and its medrese. The mosque has a fine portal; the

medrese is now the Archaeological Museum and has a collection of Hittite finds from Kültepe and Erkilet (both not far from Kayseri) as well as exhibits from the Roman, Byzantine and Seljuk periods. Behind the citadel is the covered bazaar which extends into the courtyard and arched passages of the former Vizir Hani caravanserai. The oldest mosque in Kayseri is the Great Mosque (Ulu Cami 1136–1205), a typical Seljuk pillared hall mosque. The Sahibiye Medrese (1267) houses the museum of Turkish and Islamic Art. There are four more mosques and medreses from the Seljuk period in Kayseri. Among the many türbes the Döner Kümbet (1276) is exceptionally lovely with its playfully whimsical

Atatürk Bulvari, Ankara

ornamentation and animal figures.

 Several Old Turkish hamams.

 Numerous good, typically Turkish restaurants and pie shops in the Old Town.

 To Ürgüp and the rock churches, about 75 km away.

On the road to Sivas (46 km north of Kayseri) is the magnificent and well-preserved *Sultan Hani* caravanserai (not to be confused with the caravanserai of the same name near Aksaray).

Niğde Alt. 1250 m; Pop. 40,000

Niğde is another provincial centre which is well worth a visit. The large Seljuk fortress of which there are substantial remains was built to command the passing trade route. The 15th c. Ak Medrese houses the town's archaeological museum (soon to be moved to a new building) with finds from the Niğde area. The particularly beautiful early 14th c. Hüdavent Hatun Türbesi is the mausoleum of a princess. The Sungur Bey Mosque, also 14th c., has features which betray a Mongol influence.

14 km north-west to a rock church and the Eski Gümüs monastery, decorated with fine 10th and 11th c. frescoes. 14 km south-west to the small town of Bor with its Seljuk Alâeddin Mosque and a 17th c. covered bazaar.

Ankara Alt. 840–980 m; Pop. 2.3 million

Ankara is one of the most ancient cities in Turkey and at the same time one of the most modern. What in 1923 was a small provincial town of barely 30,000, its picturesque oriental quarter crowding close round the foot of its citadel hill, has now been absorbed into the new, distinctly western metropolis with its high-rise buildings, neon lights and wide boulevards. It is in Ankara that the effects of Kemal Pasha's 'Europeanisation' of Turkey can be felt most strongly. Yet against the background of reinforced concrete buildings and city motorways the crowds thronging the commercial streets are colourfully diverse. Elegant young Turkish girls and men in western-style clothing mingle with peasant women in gay headscarves and wide breeches, while at nightfall the streets become a male preserve in accordance with eastern custom. On Atatürk Bulvari the latest fashions, cars and gadgets are sold at fixed retail prices, while in the bazaar below the citadel people still bargain over their coffee and their hubble-bubble pipes as they have since long ago.

 An ancient city

No-one knows exactly how old Ankara is. According to the latest research the Hittites settled here three and a half to four thousand years ago and many historians now support the theory that Ankara is the Hittite Ankuva (it is at least known that the Romans called the city Ancyra). Nero made it capital of the Roman province of Galatia and in the 14th c. the Ottomans renamed it Engüriye, which in Europe became 'Angora'. From this derives the expression 'Angora cat', and Ankara still abounds with cats of every possible colour.

During the Turkish War of Independence Ankara became the centre of the freedom movement and on October 13th 1923 Kemal Pasha Atatürk declared the city capital of the new Turkish Republic. After this, especially from 1928 onwards, large-scale urban building projects were initiated in which European architects and town planners participated. As yet no solution has been found to the serious problem of air pollution in the city, caused mainly by the widespread use of poor quality oil and other fuels for heating and transport.

 A stroll along Atatürk Bulvari

The very wide Atatürk Bulvari, almost 6 km long, crosses Ankara from Ulus Meydani (Ulus Square), with its equestrian statue of Atatürk, to Cankaya. On the hill at Cankaya are the Presidential Palace and Atatürk's former house (in the Palace gardens). Atatürk's tomb is in a huge mausoleum and is now a national shrine.

On any visit to Ankara time should certainly be allowed for a leisurely walk along Atatürk Bulvari. If a start is made from Ulus Meydani, the nearby Genclik Parki, a fairground park with rowing boats, mini-railway, restaurants, snack stalls and tea-gardens, is a good place to

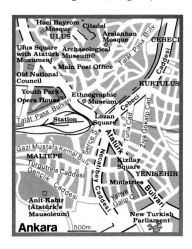

Ankara   500m

Kizilay, Güven Park and Monument, Ankara

pause and relax.

Continuing the walk leads you across the busy Lozan Meydani to Kizilay Meydani with its row of government buildings and the Confidence Monument; then on through the business district and the adjacent diplomatic quarter.

After crossing Kizilay Meydani it is worth making a detour leftwards along Meşrutiyet Caddesi and Mithatpaşa Caddesi for a visit to the impressive new Kocatepe Mosque.

Around the citadel

Visits to the citadel and the Archaeological Museum (closed on Monday, as are all the museums in Ankara) are best combined. The museum is housed in the (restored) former caravanserai and adjoining buildings of the old covered bazaar immediately below the outer fortress wall.

Somewhat confusingly the museum is referred to by three different names: the Archaeological Museum (Arkeoloji Müzesi), Hittite Museum (Hitit Müzesi) and Museum of Anatolian Civilisations. Strictly speaking 'Hittite Museum' refers only to part of the collection; the museum does indeed have a world famous Hittite department with 3000- to 4000-year old sculptures, reliefs, cuneiform tablets and small works of art from Hattuşa in particular; but it also possesses some unique items from other periods. These include Stone Age cult figures from Hacilar and Çatal Höyük, alabaster figures and pottery etc. from the Assyrian trading colony at Kültepe, and finds from the Phrygian and east Anatolian Urartian empires.

From the Archaeological Museum an alley ascends through the Hisar Gate in the lower fortress wall (5 m thick) to the main gate of the citadel, the Finger Gate (Parmak Kapisi). All of Ankara's history is reflected in its citadel walls since past lords and masters of the city have used fragments of columns, reliefs, sculptures and sills to repair and strengthen them. The views from the citadel's various terraces are magnificent. Be sure not to miss the open bazaar directly below the south-east wall, nor the Aslanhane Mosque (which incorporates fragments of more ancient buildings and has a Roman stone lion standing in the courtyard) and the Çikrikçilar Sok with its old textile shops.

The Yeni Cami designed by Sinan and the Karacabey Mosque with its beautiful portal are also well worth a visit.

If time is limited it is best to concentrate on the 15th c. Haci Bayram Mosque north-west of the citadel and the ruins of the Roman Temple of Augustus close by. Inscribed on the temple wall is a record of the Emperor Augustus' achievements which has proved immeasurably important for historical research. Even the briefest visit should leave enough time for a photograph of the nearby Julian Column (4th c. A.D.) on which storks can usually be seen nesting.

To reach the **Ethnographical Museum** from the Old Town, walk parallel to Atatürk Bulvari on its left-hand side in the direction of Lozan Meydani. The museum possesses a splendid collection of carvings (doors, prayer steps etc.), Koranic texts, miniatures, costumes, carpets and the like, unfortunately labelled only in Turkish. Close by is the so-called People's House which contains a collection of Ottoman art.

Ankara has a number of first-class hotels as well as some very acceptable middle-of-the-range ones. There is camping at the *BP Mocamp Susuzköy*, 22 km west on the main Istanbul highway, and at the *Bayindür Baraji* camping site (15 km towards Sivas).

The hotels offer Turkish specialities as well as international cuisine; the Hotel *Kent* (on the corner of Mithatpasa Caddesi and Atatürk Bulvari) is excellent for quality, price and service. There are nightclubs in the Hotels *Marmara* and *Kent* and in the roof gardens of the hotels *Büyük Ankara* and *Dedeman*.

Restaurants recommended in Ankara are: *Altin Nal Lokantasi*, Cankaya; *Restoran R.V.*, Kavaklidere; *Kristal Restoran*, Kizilay; *Hülya Restoran*, Cankaya; *Kral Ciftliğe*, Kavaklidere. *Körfez* and *Yakamoz* are taverns providing Turkish specialities and Turkish music. Also highly recommended is *Merkez Lokantasi*, a short distance out of town at Atatürk's model farm (Atatürk Orman Ciftliği).

Atatürk Mausoleum, Ankara

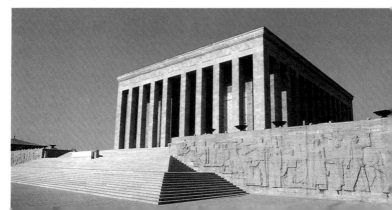

Yazilikaya, open air Hittite temple, Boğazkale

empire was ended in about 1200 B.C. by insurgent Greek and Asiatic tribes. The countless finds (including jewellery, reliefs and clay tablets) are now in Ankara's unique Museum of Anatolian Civilisations (the 'Hittite Museum'), but Hattusa itself is still worth a visit, as is the small archaeological museum in Boğazkale. The size and strength of the Hittite fortifications can be easily appreciated from the remains of the double town walls, the Royal Gate (the statue in front is a copy, the original is in Ankara), the Lion Gate and Yer Kepi, a tunnel-like entrance. Of the many temples, houses, storerooms, archives and other buildings whose foundations have been excavated, the most memorable is the Great Temple of the Lion or Weather God. A cliff face south of the hill fortress bears a badly eroded hieroglyphic-like inscription.

🚌 3 km from Boğazkale (at Yazilikaya) is a quite astonishing Hittite sanctuary (13th c. B.C.) formed by the steep sides of a natural rock gully. The rock face is carved with bas-reliefs of gods and the Hittite King Tuthaliya.

Alacahöyük This important site lies 35 km north of Boğazkale. Excavations here uncovered different levels containing artefacts from the Stone, Copper and Bronze Ages as well as the Hittite and Phrygian periods. All the significant finds are displayed in the Hittite Museum in Ankara. The most magnificent items (including gold and bronze jewellery and cult objects) came from some thirteen tombs of Hatti princes dating back to around 2300 B.C. As yet almost nothing is known about the Hatti people. Nothing of exceptional interest remains to be seen on the site apart from the Sphinx Gate with its double-headed eagle; anyone intending to visit the Ankara museum can forgo the small museum in Alacahöyük.

Sivas Alt. 1300 m; Pop. 180,000

Sivas, a provincial centre, is situated in

ℹ️ Tourist Office, Gazi Mustafa Kemal Bulvari 33.

🚌 **Gordion** (85 km west) was capital of the Phrygian Empire which under King Midas in the late 8th c. B.C. embraced almost the whole of Asia Minor. The city is also famous for its legendary Gordion knot, reputedly impossible to untie but characteristically severed by Alexander the Great with a blow of his sword.

Excavations begun in 1953 have uncovered substantial remains of two city gates, houses with mosaic pebble floors, and several royal burial mounds (tumuli), a number of the burial chambers being open to the public. Some of the grave goods are now in the small museum at Gordion while others are in the Archaeological Museum in Ankara.

Boğazkale (Hattusa)

On a karst plateau 210 km east of Ankara near the village of Boğazkale (or Boğazköy) is the excavated site of Hattusa, capital of the Hittites, whose the middle of the upland flood plain of the river Kizilirmak, 190 km north-east of Kayseri.

Lying at the intersection of major caravan routes, the town was already an important trading centre in early times and was fortified by the Romans under the Emperor Augustus. In the middle of the 11th c. it became part of the Seljuk Sultanate of Konya, being enlarged and again fortified. On the citadel hill (a fine vantage point) only the barest traces of the later period remain to be seen.

The oldest Seljuk building is the Ulu Cami (about 1100), a large pillared mosque with a lovely minaret. Further important relics of Seljuk rule are the Gök Medrese, Şifaiye Medrese and Çifte Minare Medrese (all with highly regarded, very elaborate portals, though of the latter only the façade remains); the Muzaffer Bürüciye Medrese, which houses a folklore collection; and the Abdulvahap Gazi Türbe. There are several mosques, türbes, caravanserais and baths dating from the heyday of the Ottoman Empire (14th to 16th c.)

Tokat Alt. 650 m; Pop. 180,000

This typically Turkish town involved in commerce and craftwork is largely unspoiled and offers an abundance of subjects for photographs (but take care not to cause offence when photographing people). The hill, topped by an Ottoman citadel, provides an excellent vantage point from which to look down over the old town. Among its many noteworthy old buildings are the 13th c. Gök Medrese with its arcaded courtyard and tiles, the 15th c. Beyazit Mosque, and the Voyvoda Hani (a 17th c. caravanserai). Tokat, about 100 km north of Sivas, is surrounded by orchards and vineyards, and lies in a depression between the central plateau and the mountains of the Black Sea coastal chain.

Amasya Alt. 425 m; Pop. 45,000

Steeped in history and well worth seeing, Amasya occupies a narrow valley at the south end of the Pontic Mountains, between Tokat and the Black Sea town of Samsun roughly 120 km away. The ruined citadel affords a magnificent view over the lovely town, at its most striking in the evening when lights from the houses flicker along the valley and the rock tombs (2nd c. B.C.) are illuminated. Its colourful markets are another of Amasya's attractions.

During the Greek colonial period the town was called Amaseia and was taken by the Romans shortly before the beginning of the Christian era. Under Byzantine rule it became an archbishopric. A church from this period was later converted into the Fethiye Mosque (worth visiting). Of Seljuk origin are the Burmali Minare Mosque, the Torumtay Türbe, and the beautiful Gök Medrese mosque, now a small archaeological and folklore museum (with the mummies of two Mongol rulers). There are also numerous historic buildings from the Ottoman period.

Divriği Ulu Mosque, Sivas

Useful things to know...

Before you go

Climate

When considering a holiday in Turkey in summer you must be prepared for high temperatures. In Istanbul during July and August the day temperature averages 28°–29°C; on the Black Sea coast in summer it is a couple of degrees cooler; on the Aegean coast the temperature is usually well above 30°C and on the Turkish 'Riviera' only a degree or so less. On the other hand spring and autumn can be very pleasantly warm, although there is more likelihood of rain.

What to take

The visitor to Istanbul, Ankara, Izmir or Antalya will usually be able to find almost everything needed during a stay; but even here certain makes of film may not always be available, especially film for movie cameras. Films cost about the same in Turkey as they do in the UK.

First-aid kit: It is advisable to take a supply of essential remedies with you, especially any medicines which you regularly use at home. You should also take something to treat the more everyday ailments such as stomach upsets, headaches, colds etc. which can strike at any time. Language difficulties and lack of even the most common medications are likely to create problems for anyone forced to shop at a Turkish chemist.

Holiday accommodation

Turkey has five categories of hotel: luxury (H-L) and first class (H1), and second to fourth class tourist hotels (H2 to H4). First class motels (M1) are similar in standard to H1 and H2 hotels, M2 motels to H2 and H3 hotels. The price of all accommodation is set by the State.

In the past few years many new holiday villages have been built in Turkey offering bungalow accommodation with restaurants and sports and other facilities. The cheap private pensions and youth hostels can also be recommended.

Campers and those touring with their own caravans will find all amenities (e.g. barbecues, showers, washrooms and shops) at reasonable prices in the BP Mocamps.

Whatever sort of accommodation you decide upon it is important to book early for the peak holiday period and for Istanbul at any time. Single rooms are rare.

Insurance

It is advisable to take out special medical insurance covering the period of your visit as well as insuring your luggage and personal effects.

Getting to Turkey

By air: There are scheduled flights from London, Bristol, Birmingham, Manchester and Newcastle to Istanbul, Dalaman, Izmir and Antalya, as well as charter flights and package tours to the main resorts. Schoolchildren and students travelling to and within Turkey with Turkish airlines (THY) can claim a 60 per cent discount.

By rail: Because of the distance involved travelling by rail from Great Britain to Turkey can mean a very tedious journey. Services run from Dortmund and Munich (Germany), Venice (Italy) and Vienna (Austria). There is no rail bridge over the Bosporus so anyone travelling to Asiatic Turkey must change stations in Istanbul.

By road: It is over 3000 km by road to Istanbul. The best route is via Brussels and Frankfurt to Belgrade and then on to either Sofia and Edirne or to Skopje, Thessalonika and Ipsala. From Frankfurt to Belgrade there is a choice between the route via Vienna and Budapest or the alternative via Munich, Villach and Zagreb. Although there are no direct coach services from Great Britain to Istanbul there are Eurobus services from Munich, Vienna and Geneva and services operated by Turkish companies from Paris.

Immigration and Customs Regulations

For a stay of up to three months UK nationals need only a valid passport.

Customs: Normally only a verbal declaration is required on arrival and departure but details of any precious metals, precious stones or similar items of value should be recorded in the owner's passport on entry. Cameras, one radio, one record player and other personal effects can be taken into Turkey duty-free as can up to 400 cigarettes or 50 cigars, and up to 5 litres of alcohol.

No weapons or sharp instruments (not even camping knives) may be taken into the country and the import of narcotics of all kinds is prohibited. Trading in and consuming narcotics carries heavy penalties in Turkey.

Gifts (jewellery, leather goods, etc.) to the value of £150 need not be declared on entry. Souvenirs exceeding this value may be taken out of the country duty-free provided the appropriate currency exchange slips are produced.

The export of antiquities from Turkey is absolutely prohibited. A certificate of authorisation issued by a museum is required before an old carpet or other antique item can be taken out.

Vehicle documents: Details of any vehicle must be recorded in your passport before entry and vehicles must leave the country within three months. It is advisable to take the vehicle registration certificate with you to prove that nothing has been changed on your vehicle whilst in Turkey.

Should you wish to visit another country during your stay, taking a boat trip to Greece or Cyprus for example, your car must be left at the local Customs Office where it will placed under customs seal.

You will need an international driving licence and international insurance certificate (Green Card) endorsed for both European and Asiatic Turkey. Turkish third party insurance can be arranged if necessary at the frontier posts. Information for motorists can be obtained from the Turkish Tourism and Information Office in London (see page 94) and from RAC Touring Services Dept.; tel. 01 686 2525.

During your stay

Currency

The unit of currency is the Turkish lira (TL). There are banknotes in denominations of 10, 20, 50, 100, 500, 1000, 5000, and 10,000 TL as well as 5, 10, and 50 TL coins. The value of the currency changes continuously because of the Turkish inflation rate. Generally speaking a better exchange rate is available in Turkey than is offered by UK banks.

Current exchange rates can be found in the national press, or obtained from banks or the RAC.

There is no limit put on the amount of Turkish currency taken into Turkey but on leaving only currency to a value of $1000 may be taken out. The import of sterling and other foreign currencies is also unrestricted but there is again a limit to the amount which may be taken out, in this case not exceeding the value of the foreign currency taken in. Currency declarations must be made on entry and departure.

There are exchange facilities at frontier posts, in banks and saving banks and in hotels licensed for the purpose. Travellers cheques and Eurocheques are subject to the usual conditions. Be sure to keep all your exchange slips since without them it is impossible to change money back into sterling. The duty-free shops only accept foreign currencies. Beware of street traders illegally offering advantageous exchange rates. Many a visitor has realized too late that he has been swindled, the genuine notes having been swopped at lightning speed for worthless paper! Be sure also to maintain a good supply of small change (obtained from the bank if necessary).

Electricity

The voltage is 220 volts, 50 cycles AC, though a very few small villages are still on 110 volts. Plugs are standard European 2-pin type. Adaptors are not readily available so take a suitable one with you.

Festivals and Public Holidays

In contrast to other Islamic countries, Sunday in Turkey is the official day of rest. Two Islamic feasts, the Sugar Festival and the Festival of the Sacrifice, are observed (no fixed dates) but the Christian festivals of Christmas, Easter, etc. are not.

New Year: January 1st.

National Independence Day, also Children's Day: April 23rd.

Atatürk's Remembrance Day, also Youth and Sports Day: May 19th.

Victory Day: August 30th.

Republic Day (Anniversary of the founding of the Turkish Republic): October 29th.

Newspapers

English newspapers are usually available in the large holiday resorts the day after printing. The English-language 'Daily News' published in Turkey is available just about everywhere.

Opening times

Banks and offices are usually open Monday to Friday 8.30 a.m. to 12 noon and 1.30 p.m. to 5 or 5.30 p.m. In some places the Ministry of Tourism Information Bureaux are also open on Sunday during the peak holiday period.

Shops are normally open Monday to Saturday 9 a.m. to 1 p.m. and 2 p.m. to 7 p.m.

Post and Telephone

Main Post Offices are open from 8 a.m. to midnight, others from 8 a.m. to 8 p.m. (closing for lunch). They are not open on Sunday. Stamps are sold in some souvenir shops and hotels as well as at post-offices. (Details of postal charges are not given here since they change frequently.)

To make a call from a public telephone box you will need jettons (tokens) which can be bought in post offices or at a nearby shop. Long-distance calls can be dialled direct.

Religious services

The only Catholic or Protestant church services are in Istanbul, Izmir or Ankara. Istanbul also has a synagogue.

Restaurants

In most hotel restaurants the food is good and reasonably priced, with a selection ranging from Turkish specialities to Wiener Schnitzel. A menu is displayed outside each restaurant. In the nightclubs prices are about five times as high as elsewhere.

Souvenirs

Since its earliest days Turkey has been engaged in trading between east and west and even today it retains something of the character of a huge bazaar. Every conceivable type of craftwork, from embroidery, handwoven fabrics, ceramics, copper and brassware to articles made from meerschaum, onyx and wood, as well as gold and silver jewellery, hand-knotted carpets, all manner of leather goods, extremely sweet, brightly coloured liqueurs, candied fruits and a great variety of Turkish delight can all be bought at reasonable prices. The attractive brochures to be found in the shops run by the Ministry of Culture and Tourism are an excellent guide to the rich selection of goods available.

Time

Turkey observes Eastern European Time which is two hours ahead of Greenwich Mean Time. From April to September it is three hours ahead of GMT.

Tipping

It is customary to tip about 10 per cent in restaurants. Elsewhere a certain amount of discretion is needed in deciding whether to tip or not; some staff — tourist guides for example — might in some circumstances be offended by the offer of money.

Traffic regulations

Generally speaking Turkish traffic signs and traffic regulations conform to international protocol. Even on the main highways however the road is shared with cows, sheep and other four-legged animals and at night unlit vehicles are not uncommon.

It is essential to drive extremely carefully wherever you are in Turkey. Being involved in an accident can have very serious consequences. The police must be informed of accidents even if nobody is injured since Turkish insurance companies insist on a police report. In the case of injury to a person the driver involved will usually be taken straight into custody. Should this happen, contact the British Consul immediately.

In the event of breakdown the Turkish Touring and Automobile Club provides assistance free of charge to members of international automobile clubs. Vehicle repair workshops are only to be found in towns and on the principal highways but a Turkish village smith will often prove himself a master of improvisation, going to any amount of trouble to a put a car to rights.

Petrol is cheaper than in the UK. The only grades available are Regular 91 octane and Super 96 octane. Turkey has a comparatively large number of filling stations.

Transport in Turkey

Air services

Turkish Airlines (THY) operate frequent domestic services, especially from Istanbul to Ankara and Izmir. Most inland flights begin and end at Istanbul and nearly all routes are served by modern jets. Prices tend to be lower than in the UK but there is no saving on return journeys.

Buses

Bus fares are exceptionally cheap and there is a very extensive network of services, but the heat and the sometimes poor roads mean that long journeys by bus are not always very pleasurable.

Car hire

Most of the important car hire firms have offices in Istanbul, Ankara, Izmir, Kuşadasi, Marmaris and other major Turkish towns. The addresses of local car hire firms can be obtained from the tourist and information offices when you arrive in Turkey.

On the whole towns, villages and tourist attractions are amply and clearly signposted, as are the numerous mostly very pleasant rest and picnic places. Nevertheless a good road map is essential. The Turkish Tourism and Information Office in London (see page 94) can supply plans of the larger towns.

Ferries

Information about ferry services on the Black Sea, Sea of Marmara, Mediterranean and Dardanelles is available from the Turkish Maritime Lines offices in Istanbul, Izmir and Ankara.

Railways

Travel by Turkey's domestic rail service tends to be a slow business, express trains (some with dining and sleeping cars) running on only a few main line routes.

Turkish handicraft

Taxis

In all the major towns taxis are plentiful and can be recognised by a black/yellow band. If a taxi does not have a meter, it is advisable to agree the fare in advance.

Shared taxis (dolmus) run between the smaller places. Their prices vary according to distance but on the whole are comparable to a bus fare.

Important addresses

Diplomatic and Consular Offices
In U.K.

Turkish Embassy
43 Belgrave Square,
London SW1; tel. (01) 235 5252.
In Turkey
British Embassy
Şehit Ersan Caddesi 46A,
Çankaya, Ankara; tel. 27 43 10.

British Consulate
Meşrutiyet Caddesi 34,
Tepebaşi, Istanbul; tel. 1 44 75 45.

1442 Sokak 49/51
Alsancak, Izmir; tel. 21 17 95.

Tourist Information Offices
In U.K.
Turkish Tourist Office
170 Piccadilly,
London W1V 9DD; tel. (01) 734 8681.

In Turkey
Local Tourist Offices

Alanya: Carşi Mah. Kalearkasi Cad.
Ankara: Gazi Mustafa Kemal Bul. 33.
Antalya: Cumhuriyet Cad. 91.
Bodrum: 12 Eylül Meydani.
Bursa: Saydam Is Merkezi 21.
Edirne: Talatpasa Asfalti 76/A.
Istanbul: Divan Yolu Cad. 3.
        Karaköy Yolcu Salonu.
        Hilton Hotel.
        Yeşilköy Airport.
Izmir: Büyük Efes Hotel.
Kuşadasi: Iskele Meydani.
Marmaris: Iskele Meydani 39.
Ürgüp: Kayseri Cad. 37.

English, French and/or German are normally spoken by staff at the above Tourist Offices.

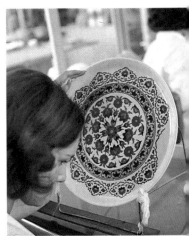

Porcelain decoration

Useful words and phrases

As it is written and spoken today, Turkish is a young language, having been formed after the founding of the Republic in 1923. The Latin alphabet has been used since 1928, with the addition of a few diacritic marks, notably the cedilla under 'ç' and 's', umlauts on ö and ü, the hacek over ğ and ocasionally a circumflex on â. One unique feature is the dotless ı in addition to the ordinary i; (capital İ always has a dot). The ı and I are not shown in the text of this book.

Pronunciation is not too difficult for English speakers. Vowels are always pronounced short (e.g. 'a' as in hat, 'e' as in pet, 'i' as in hit, 'o' as in hot and 'u' as in hut; 'ö' is like the 'eu' in the French word deux and 'ü' has the sound of une in French. The dotless ı has a somewhat indefinite sound, something akin to the vowel sound in ugh.

Consonants are pronounced much as in English with the following exceptions:- 'c' = j, 'ç' like ch in 'church', 'g' merely lengthens the preceeding vowel sound, 'h' is always clearly aspirated and often sounds like the 'ch' in the Scottish word loch. 'j' has the sound of the 's' in treasure, 's' = 'sh'. Words are almost always stressed on the final syallable.

In tourist areas French can often serve as a means of communication; many — especially the younger generation — also speak English. A great number of Turks have worked in Germany and many speak German quite well. However, a few words of Turkish may well prove useful and any attempt to communicate with the people in their own language will be warmly welcomed.

(in the following short selection the dotless ı has been shown)

please	lütfen	0 sıfır
thank you	teşekkür ederim	1 bir
yes /no	evet / hayır	2 iki
excuse me	affedersiniz	3 üç
do you speak English ?	Ingilizce billiyor musunuz?	4 dört
Good day	merhaba	5 beş
Good evening	akşamınız hayırli olsun	6 altı
Good night	geceniz haırli olsun	7 yedi
Goodbye	Allaha ısmarladik	8 sekiz
how much ?	bunun fıatı nedir?	9 dokuz
I should like	.... istiyorum	10 on
open	açik	11 on bir
shut	kapanıyor	12 on iki
where is ....?	nerededir....?	20 yirmi
left	sola	50 elli
right	sağa	100 yüz
straight on	dosdoğru	
post office	postane	
bank	banka	
railway station	istasyon	
police station	polis karakolu	
information office	danışma (istihbarat)	
doctor	hekım	
chemist	eczane	
toilet	tuvalet (helâ)	
ladies	bayanlar (kadın)	
gentlemen	baylar (erkek)	
entrance	giriş	
exit	çikiş	

Index

Adana	72	Catal Höyük	78
Adrianople (see Edirne)		Çavuşin	82
Afyon	75	Çekirge	36
Agri Daği (see Ararat)		Çengelköy	31
Aizani	75	Çeşme	5, 48
Akalissos	64	Chalcedon	13
Akçakoca	40	Chimaera	64
Akçay	43	Constantinople	11, 14, 16, 22
Aksaray	78	Çubuklu	32
Akşehir	78	Çukurova (plain)	71
Alacahöyük	88	Dalyan	57
Alanya	5, **68ff**	Damlataş (cave)	69
Amasra	40	Dardanelles	38
Amasya	89	Dardanos	38
Amisos (see Samsum)		Datça	57
Anadolu Hisari	32	Demre	63
Anadolu Kavagi	32	Derinkuyu	80
Anamur	70	Didim (see Didyma)	
Anamurion (see Anamur)		Didyma	4, 52, 53
Anazarbus	72	Dikili	43
Ankara	5, 6, 15, **85ff**	Düden (waterfall)	66
Antakya	73	Edirne	11, 16, 20
Antalya	5, **64f**	Edremit	43
Antioch (see Hatay)		Eğridir	76
Aphrodisias	4, 60	Emirgân	32
Ararat	6	Ephesus	4, **49ff**
Arnavutköy	32	Erciyes Daği	5, 78, 82
Aslankaya	75	Erdek	33
Aslantaş	75	Euromos	56
Aspendos	4, 67	Fethiye	42, 57
Ataköy	33	Finike	63
Avanos	82	Florya	33
Avcilar	80	Foça	45
Avşar Ad. (island)	33	Fort Yuşa	32
Ayvacik	43	Gallipoli	31
Babaeski	20	Gelibolu	38
Bebek	32	Giresun	40
Belceğiz (bay)	59	Golden Horn	21, 26
Bergama	43, 45	Gordion	88
Beşiktaş	31	Gökova (gulf)	56
Beykoz (bay)	32	Göreme	80
Beylerbeyi	31	Gülşehir	80
Beyşehir	76	Gümüldür	48
Bodrum	5, **54ff**	Hacibektaş	80
Boğazkale	11, 88	Hacilar	74
Boğazköy (see Boğazkale)		Halikarnassos (see Bodrum)	
Bosporus	21, **31ff**	Hasandaği	5
Bekoz (bay)	32	Hatay	73
Burdur	74	Hattuşa	11
Burgaz Ada	33	Herakleia	53
Bursa	5, 11, 16, **33ff**	Heybeli Ada	33
Büyük Ada	33	Hierapolis	4, 59, **60**
Büyükdere	31, 32	Incekum	68
Byzantium (see		Insuyu (cave)	74
Constantinople)		Iskenderun	73
Çanakkale	31, 42	Isparta	76
Cappadocia	4, **78f**	Istanbul	5, 6, 11, 16, 19, **21ff**
Istinyie	32	Ören	43
Istranca (mountains)	19	Özkonak	82
Izmir	4, **46f**	Pamukkale	5, **59f**
Iznik	37f	Paradise Grotto	71
Kadirli	73	Paşabahçe	32
Kalkan	62	Pasalimani Ad. (island)	33
Kandilli	32	Pergamon	4, 12, **43f**
Kanlica	32	Perge	4, 66
Kanlidivane	71	Phaselis	63
Kanytellis (see Kanlidivane)		Priene	4, 52
Kara Ada	56	Princes' Islands	31, 32
Karagöl	63	Rhodiapolis	64
Karaman	78	Rize	40
Karatepe	72, 73	Rumeli Hisari	32
Kaş	5, 61	Rumeli Kavagi	32
Kaunos	57	Sagalassos	76
Kaymakli	80	Samsun	40, 41
Kayseri	82	Saraylice (island)	21
Kekov Ad. (island)	62	Sardis	47
Kemer	5, 63	Sariyer	32
Kilyos	40	Sea of Marmara	31, 32, 33
Kinali Ada	33	Seferihisar	47
Knidos	57	Selçuk	49
Konya	11, 14, 16, **76ff**	Seyitgazi	76
Kormos	64	Side	4, 67f
Korydalla	64	Sigacik	47
Korykos	71	Şile	40
Köroğludaği	5	Silifke	71
Köyceğiz	57	Sille	78
Kuşadasi	5, 48	Sinop	40, 41
Kültepe	86	Sirens' Isle	46
Limyra	63	Sivas	88
Lüleburgaz	20	Smyrna (see Izmir)	
Malazgirt	11	Soğanli	82
Manavgat	68	Tarabya	32
Manisa	47	Tarsus	72
Manzikert (see Malazgirt)		Tekirdag	20
Marmara Ad. (island)	33	Teos	47
Marmaris	57	Termessos	4, 66
Mavrucan	82	Tokat	89
Meram	78	Trabzon	40
Meriç	19	Trebizond (see Trabzon)	
Mersin	71f	Troy	4, 38f
Midas Şehri	75	Tuz Gölü (salt lake)	74
Miletos (see Miletus)		Uchisar	80
Miletus	4, 52	Ulu Dağ	5, 33, 36f
Misis	72	Urla	47
Mudanya	33	Ürgüp	80
Muğla	59	Vaniköy	32
Mut	71	Xanthos	4, 62
Myra (see Demre)		Yalova	33
Nevşehir	79	Yeniköy	32
Niğde	84	Yenimahalle	32
Ölü Deniz	59	Yeşilköy	33
Olympos	64	Zelve	82
Ortahisar	80	Zonguldak	40
Ortaköy	31		